WRESTLING *With* LIFE

Lessons from the Story of Jacob

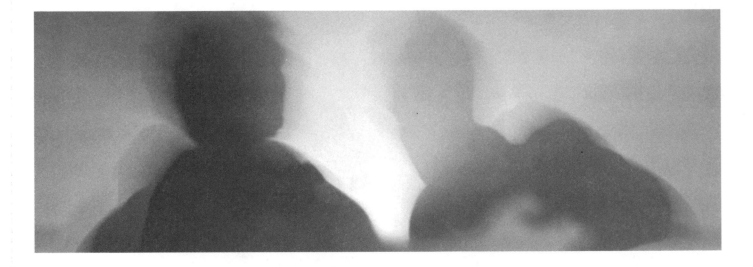

Genesis 25-50

BY BOB BULLER

STANDARD
PUBLISHING
Cincinnati, Ohio

TABLE of CONTENTS

All Scripture quotations, unless otherwise indicated, are taken from the HOLY BIBLE, NEW INTERNATIONAL VERSION®. NIV®. Copyright © 1973, 1978, 1984 by International Bible Society. Used by permission of Zondervan Publishing House. All rights reserved.

Cover design by
Steve Diggs & Friends

Inside design by
Liz Howe Design
Cover photo by
PhotoDisc

Edited and developed by
Jim Eichenberger

©1999 by The Standard Publishing Company
All rights reserved.
Printed in the U.S.A.

Solid Foundation is
an imprint from
The Standard Publishing
Company, Cincinnati, Ohio.
A division of Standex
International Corporation.

06 05 04 03 02 01 00 99
5   4   3   2   1

HOW TO USE THIS BOOK

Your adult Sunday school class or Bible study probably contains people of different personalities from diverse backgrounds and with varying levels of biblical knowledge. *WRESTLING WITH LIFE—Lessons From the Story of Jacob* is designed to equip you to teach biblical truths in ways that will reach every member of your class, regardless of his or her personality or background.

Each lesson contains valuable information to help you prepare your lesson. Pay special attention to the lesson title. It has been carefully crafted to communicate the main point of the study. This is the biblical truth that you want people to learn during the lesson and then apply during the days and weeks to come. Next, read the **Lesson Objectives.** They explain how the lesson will encourage people to discover and apply the main point of the study to their own lives. Finally, use the **Scripture Commentary** to deepen your own understanding of God's Word. The insights and biblical background within this section will prepare you to teach God's Word just as you would like—with excellence and with confidence.

Furthermore, the body of each lesson has been carefully constructed to take students where they are and then lead them into a discovery and personal application of the truths of God's Word. To accomplish this, each lesson body contains the following three sections:

Getting a hold . . . This opening activity introduces learners to the lesson topic and whets their appetites for the biblical content to follow. Use it to focus students' minds on the issue at hand and to open their hearts to receive God's truths.

Taking it to the mat . . . This is the heart of the lesson, a time for meaningful study of God's Word. Best of all, studying the Bible doesn't have to be dull, as you will soon discover when you use the varied learning activities provided by this book.

Pinning it down . . . Bible study profits little if it makes no difference in people's daily lives. So each lesson concludes with a time of personal application. Invite learners to apply what they've learned right away. You'll be excited at how much more they learn—and what a difference it makes in their lives.

One of those application activities for each lesson is "The Follow-Through Factor." This reproducible take-home devotional guide will allow your learners to more fully explore the relevance of the lesson throughout the following week.

Finally, each lesson offers a number of learning activities that you can match to the different learning styles of your class members. The people in your group do not all learn in the same way, so you need to provide various types of learning activities in each lesson.

That's why each lesson in this book offers a number of learning activities for you to choose from. In fact, each section of every lesson provides two options so you can choose the best possible activity for your particular group. In short, you can custom-design a lesson for your group.

You have the tools, so why wait? Prepare lessons that are uniquely your own. Lead your group in an enjoyable and effective study of the Word of God.

LESSON 1

Jacob struggled with his relationships to his parents and his brother.

LESSON SCRIPTURE

Genesis 25:19-34; 27:1-45; 32:1–33:17

SCRIPTURE COMMENTARY

The book of Genesis tells us the story of Jacob, a man born to struggles if ever there was one. Jacob's family life presented him with particular difficulty.

Jacob struggled with labels and expectations placed on him at birth—Jacob's family struggles began before he was ever born. From the moment that God told Rebekah that the older of the twins in her womb (Esau) would serve the younger (Jacob), conditions were ripe for family conflict (Genesis 25:23).

Though the Bible does not say so explicitly, one might assume that Jacob learned of his favored status early in life and that it colored the way he looked at his brother and himself. Jacob may have grown up with the idea that he was to receive every blessing that his family had to bestow.

This would explain in some measure Jacob's "grasping" at various family rights: his purchase of Esau's right to a larger inheritance and his deceptive pilfering of the blessing intended for his brother (Genesis 25:29-34; 27:1-29). Jacob seemed to believe that God's prenatal pronouncement authorized him to do whatever was necessary to seize what was rightfully his.

In short, Jacob's expectations of family favor and his apparent acceptance of the "grasper" label created various struggles within his family. Instead of recognizing that the promised blessing could come only from God, Jacob sought to take it from others. It is only when Jacob struggled to gain his blessing from God (Genesis 32:22-32) that he ceased his own devious attempts to seize what had been promised him before he was ever born.

Jacob struggled with imperfect, manipulative parents—Jacob's expectations and family role were not the sole cause of his problems. The attitudes and actions of his parents compounded the situation.

First, each parent showed favoritism to one of the twins: Isaac, who had a taste for wild game, loved Esau the skillful hunter; Rebekah loved Jacob (Genesis 25:28). The Bible does not explain why Rebekah loved Jacob, but the context might suggest that her favoring of Jacob derived from her knowledge of his future (Genesis 25:23).

Lesson Objectives

In the course of this lesson, students will
- recall childhood memories in order to identify family problems they experienced.
- describe how Jacob encountered and handled difficulties in his childhood.
- consider how one would follow Jacob's example in family situations today

In time, this parental favoritism erupted into preferential treatment. Isaac, following the custom of his day, planned to bestow a special blessing on his firstborn son, on Esau (Genesis 27:1-4). This blessing would ensure both Esau's prosperity and his preeminence over his brother.

Why wasn't Jacob the intended recipient of his father's blessing? It could be that Isaac was unaware of Rebekah's revelation or that this parental blessing and God's promised favor were not one and the same. It is also possible that Isaac cared little about what God had decreed and preferred to establish the supremacy of his favorite son, the one who sated his hunger for wild game.

When Rebekah heard of Isaac's intention, she countered it with a deceptive plan of her own. In the end, Jacob fooled his father into giving him the blessing (Genesis 27:5-17), but these parental maneuvers and manipulations left a permanent scar on the entire family. Isaac was angry with Jacob (27:33), Esau wanted to kill Jacob (27:41), and eventually Jacob left his mother behind, never to see her again (27:42–28:5).

Jacob struggled with sibling rivalry and hostility—As we have already observed, Jacob's biggest family struggle was with his twin brother, Esau. Twice Jacob struggled to wrest from Esau the rights that Jacob believed were his. First Jacob took advantage of his brother's weakness to get Esau's right to the family inheritance (Genesis 25:29-34), then Jacob took advantage of his father's age to steal the blessing Isaac had meant for Esau (27:18-40). Because Jacob cared only about his own interests, he damaged his relationship with Esau to the point that Jacob had to flee his family to save his life (27:41-45).

Eventually, however, Jacob overcame his sibling struggles, and the two brothers managed to live out their days in peace. How Jacob accomplished this shows us how we too can mend broken family relationships even today.

Most important, Jacob met God face-to-face and renewed his relationship with his heavenly Father (Genesis 32:22-32). Jacob had manipulated, taken advantage of, and deceived others because he apparently did not trust God to keep his promise. When Jacob struggled with God, however, he not only gained God's blessing but also was enabled to restore relations with his brother.

Jacob's restoration plan contained two important elements. First, Jacob humbled himself before Esau, claiming that Esau was his "lord" and that he, Jacob, was Esau's "servant" (Genesis 32:4, 5, 18, 20; 33:5, 13, 14; cf. 33:3). Second, Jacob took specific steps (the giving of presents) to restore his relationship with his estranged brother (32:13-21; 33:8-11). Once Jacob realized that God would keep his promise to honor Jacob, he ceased grasping at what Esau had and began to humbly give what he had to Esau.

Like Jacob, Christians today struggle with difficult and damaged family relations. But as the story of Jacob shows, God can heal and restore those broken relationships if we place our trust in him and humbly do what we can to mend the wounds of the past. ✧

Hebrew Helps

One might even suggest that Jacob's name (which means "he follows at the heel" or "he grasps" in Hebrew) contributed to his more negative personality traits. The Hebrew word on which his name is based, "aqab" and words grammatically related to it ("iqqesh," "aqeb," "aqob," and "oqbah") are translated consistently with negative overtones. They are found in Jeremiah's pronouncement that the human heart is incurably "deceitful" (Jeremiah 17:9), in the description of Jehu acting "deceptively" to slaughter the priests of Baal (2 Kings 10:19), and also in the "ambush" of the city of Ai (Joshua 8:13). Even in modern English, a contemptible person is labeled a "heel." Certainly carrying that moniker for life would not be an asset!

GETTING A HOLD . . .

Use one of the following activities to prompt students to recall childhood memories in order to identify family problems they experienced.

Family Roles

Time: 7-10 minutes

Before class, write the following phrases on individual sheets of newsprint and hang them in different areas of the room:

- **the "obedient child"**
- **the "peacemaker"**
- **the "family joker"**
- **the "forgotten child"**
- **the "disobedient child"**

As people arrive, invite them to read all the signs and then stand by the one that best describes their family role while they were growing up.

When everyone is standing by a sign, have students share with their group members thirty-second stories that illustrate how they fit that category. Allow several minutes for discussion, then have people discuss the following questions within their groups. After each question, ask for volunteers to summarize their groups' responses. Use the sample responses which follow to help spur the thinking of the groups as necessary.

- **What were the advantages of playing this role in your family?**
  drew attention, brought rewards, gave a sense of power
- **What were the disadvantages of playing this role in your family?**
  brought punishment, caused resentment, developed a reputation
- **How did playing this role affect your relationship with your siblings?** *looked upon as a leader, viewed as a scapegoat*
- **How did playing this role affect your relationship with your parents?** *(not) suspected when trouble occurred, overnurtured, undernurtured*
- **How is this childhood role a positive force in your life as an adult?**
- **How is this childhood role a negative force in your life as an adult?**

Then lead into the Bible study by reading or restating the following in your own words: **"Every family has its good points and its bad points, its great times and its hard times. This is undoubtedly true of everyone here, but it was no less true for families in the Bible. Jacob, for example, struggled in his relationships with his parents and his brother, but he persevered through those struggles and eventually made peace with his past. Let's see what we can learn from Jacob's experiences so we can make sure that our family relationships are the best that they can possibly be."**

Family Matters

Time: 10-12 minutes

As people arrive, hand each person a copy of the "Family Matters" puzzle and

---

Materials Needed

- markers, sheets of newsprint or poster board, masking tape

Leader's Tip

Be sensitive to the different family situations from which class members may have come. Some learners may have grown up in foster homes or single-parent homes, while others may have endured physical, emotional, or sexual abuse at home. Be careful not to assume that every class member came from a "traditional" or even healthy family.

Materials Needed

- Bibles, one photocopy of the "Family Matters" handout from page 11 for each person, pencils

a pencil. Suggest that learners work together in pairs or small groups to complete the puzzle.

When everyone has arrived, allow several more minutes for students to complete the puzzle. Then ask for volunteers to read their answers. The correct answers to the puzzle are: 1) *parents;* 2) *husband, wife, children;* 3) *happy;* 4) *Adam, Eve, Cain, Abel;* 5) *killed;* 6) *arrows.*

When people transfer these answers to the puzzle, they will recreate the following quote from Leo Tolstoy: *Happy families are all alike; every unhappy family is unhappy in its own way.* If necessary, read the quote and then ask the entire class, **"What do you think Tolstoy meant by this quote? To what extent do you agree with it? Why? To what extent do you disagree with it? Explain."**

Encourage several responses to each question, then have people form groups of three or four and each tell about a time their family was a happy one. Allow several minutes for sharing, then ask the entire class: **"What was it that made your family happy at this time?"** Invite several responses, then have group members each tell about a time their family was an unhappy one. After several minutes, ask the entire class, **"What was it that made your family unhappy at this time?"**

Allow time for several responses, then lead into the Bible study by reading or restating the following in your own words: **"Every family has its happy times and its sad times, its fond recollections and its haunting memories. This is no doubt true of everyone here, and it was no less true for families in the Bible. Jacob, for example, spent much of his life plagued by family discord, but he overcame that struggle and eventually made peace with his past. Let's see what we can learn from Jacob's experiences so we can make sure that our family relationships are the best that they can possibly be."**

TAKING IT TO THE MAT . . .

Use one of the following activities to help learners describe how Jacob encountered and handled difficulties in his childhood.

Biblical Prescriptions

Time: 15-18 minutes

Have learners form groups of four or five. Encourage people to form groups with those who are not part of their families. Give each person a copy of the "Family Relations" handout and a pencil, and each group a photocopy of the **Scripture Commentary.**

Explain that group members are therapists who have been asked to examine Jacob's relationships with his family members and with God in order to discover *why* he experienced family difficulties and *how* he overcame them. Specifically, each

Materials Needed

↝ *Bibles, one photocopy of the "Family Relations" handout from page 12 for each person, photocopies of* **the Scripture Commentary,** *pencils*

group needs to list the symptoms (or external evidences) of all the problems they see, to diagnose the real problems that caused the symptoms, and to identify the biblical prescriptions that enabled Jacob to overcome these problems.

If everyone understands the task, assign each group one of these relationships to examine: Jacob and his parents, Jacob and his brother, Jacob and his God. Be sure at least one group is working on each relationship, then tell group members that they have seven minutes to complete their analyses.

While people work, circulate from group to group answering any questions, offering suggestions, and reminding people of the time remaining.

After seven minutes, ask group members to report what they discovered about Jacob and his relationships. After the groups have reported, ask the entire class the following questions. Comment as needed to bring out the main point of the lesson.

- **To what extent were Jacob's family members responsible for the problems?**
- **To what extent was Jacob responsible for the problems?**
- **How did Jacob's changed relationship with God affect his relationships with his family members?** *When Jacob focused on God's blessing, he stopped trying to grasp human blessings. This enabled him to meet and be restored to his brother. It may have been too late for Jacob to be restored to his parents.*
- **What could Jacob do to change his family members?** *Nothing.*
- **What did he do to change himself?** *He trusted God to give him what he had been struggling for; he humbled himself before Esau; he took the initiative to make amends with Esau.*

Lead into the next section of the lesson by reading or restating the following in your own words: **"Like Jacob, every one of us struggles with family problems from time to time. Some of them are caused by others; some are brought on by ourselves. And although we can't change our family members and how they treat us, we can change ourselves. Like Jacob, we can trust God to do what is right and then humbly do what *we* can to restore our family relationships to all that they can be. Let's close our time together by committing ourselves to following Jacob's example within our own families."**

Different Stories

Time: 18-20 minutes

Before class, make one photocopy of the **Scripture Commentary** for every four people. Then write the following names and Scripture references on the sheet of newsprint and hang it at the front of the room: **Rebekah (Genesis 25:21-28; 27:1-17, 41-46), Isaac (Genesis 25:27, 28; 27:1-40), Esau (Genesis 25:27-34; 27:30-41), and Jacob (Genesis 25:27-34; 27:41-46).**

Have people form groups of four or five. Give each group a copy of the

Materials Needed

⇨ Bibles, photocopies of the **Scripture Commentary**, newsprint, masking tape, a marker, pencils, paper

Scripture Commentary, paper, and a pencil. Assign each group one of the following characters: Rebekah, Isaac, Esau, and Jacob.

Explain that group members are to write a one-minute monologue explaining why there were problems within Jacob's family. Using their assigned Scriptures and the information in the **Scripture Commentary,** groups are to construct a monologue that represents the likely perspective of their character. Groups have ten minutes to prepare their monologues.

Circulate from group to group while people work, answering questions, offering suggestions, and reminding people of the time remaining. Guide the discussions as necessary to make sure they include the following perspectives:

- **Rebekah: Isaac wanted to give Jacob's rightful blessing to Esau.**
- **Isaac: Jacob deceived me to get the blessing I meant for Esau.**
- **Esau: Jacob took what was mine on two different occasions.**
- **Jacob: Esau tried to get what God had intended me to have.**

After ten minutes, invite groups to read their monologues. Then ask the entire class to evaluate the validity of the various perspectives. Allow several minutes for discussion, then ask group members to read Genesis 32:22–33:11 to discover the real source of the problem and to learn how that problem was solved.

After groups finish reading, ask the entire class the following questions:

- **What do you think was the real source of the problems in this family?** *They all sought their own interests instead of seeking the interests of others and trusting God to do what was right.*
- **In what ways did Jacob contribute to these problems?** *He manipulated and lied to get what he thought was rightfully his; he didn't trust God to keep his word.*
- **How did Jacob's changed relationship with God affect his relationships with his family members?** *When Jacob focused on God's blessing, he stopped trying to grasp human blessings. This enabled him to meet and be restored to his brother.*
- **What could Jacob do to change his family members?** *Nothing.*
- **What did he do to change himself?** *He trusted God to give him what he had been struggling for; he humbled himself before Esau; he took the initiative to make amends with Esau.*

Lead into the next section of the lesson by reading or restating the following in your own words: **"Like Jacob, every one of us struggles with family problems from time to time. Some of them are caused by others; some are brought on by ourselves. And although we can't change our family members and how they treat us, we can change ourselves. Like Jacob, we can trust God to do what is right and then humbly do what *we* can to restore our family relationships to all that they can be. Let's close our time together by committing ourselves to following Jacob's example within our own families."**

PINNING IT DOWN . . .

Use one or both of the following activities to encourage students to follow Jacob's example in their own family situations today.

Family Albums

Time: 12-15 minutes

Materials Needed

⊸ *paper, markers*

Ask people to describe for the class modern situations like those faced by Jacob's family. Class members can tell of problems from their own experiences or from the lives of people they know. For example, people might tell of children fighting over their parents' inheritance, parents offering financial support to one child but not to another, children deceiving their parents to get special favors, or parents using their children to battle against one another. Encourage people to describe what happened to the family when these problems arose and to explain how family relations could have been restored by following Jacob's example.

After four or five situations have been described, remind people that no one is immune from family problems and that everyone in class probably has at least one family relationship that could be improved. Give students one minute to think of one family member with whom they need a better relationship. While people are thinking, set out the paper and markers.

After a minute, invite class members to sketch pictures of their families, being sure to include the person with whom they need to improve relations.

Allow several minutes for people to sketch, then have students form groups of three or four with people other than their family members. Ask group members to use their drawings to "introduce" their families to each other and to briefly explain why they need a better relationship with the one family member. After each group member shares, other group members are to suggest specific ways that person could seek to restore health to the relationship.

After all the family situations have been discussed, groups are to close in prayer, thanking God for families and asking God to help each member do what he or she can to follow Jacob's example of restoring difficult family relationships.

Then move on to the next section or close the lesson by reminding students that we can't change family members or how they act, but we can trust God to do what is right as we step out in faith to humbly restore broken family relations.

The Follow-Through Factor

Time: 5 minutes

Materials Needed

⊸ *one copy of "The Follow-Through Factor" handout from page 13 for each person*

This section appears in every lesson in this series. This weekly devotion plan helps class members apply the Bible study throughout the coming week. You may use it immediately after the Bible study or in conjunction with the preceding activity.

Give each person a copy of the handout. Take time to briefly read through it, but do not discuss any of the questions at this time.

Close the session in prayer.

FAMILY MATTERS

Fill in the answers to the clues. Then transfer the letters to the correspondingly numbered squares in the diagram.

1.   Children, obey your _____ in the Lord (Ephesians 6:1).

   __ __ __ __ __ __ __
   1 2 3 4 5 6 7

2.   The three components of a family (Colossians 3:18-20).

   __ __ __ __ __ __ __, __ __ __ __, and __ __ __ __ __ __ __ __
   8 9 10 11 12 13 14   15 16 17 18   19 20 21 22 23 24 25 26

3.   What Leah was called after she bore Asher (Genesis 30:13).

   __ __ __ __ __
   27 28 29 30 31

4.   First family in the Bible (Genesis 4:1, 2).

   __ __ __ __, __ __ __, __ __ __ __, and __ __ __ __
   32 33 34 35 36 37 38 39 40 41 42   43 44 45 46

5.   What the third person named above did to the fourth (Genesis 4:8).

   __ __ __ __ __ __
   47 48 49 50 51 52

6.   What children are like in the hands of a warrior (Psalm 127:4).

   __ __ __ __ __ __
   53 54 55 56 57 58

■						■								■
■	20	12	29	1	31	■	17	28	35	48	22	21	18	58	■
■				■		■		■						■
■		2	54	38	■	32	50	22	■	34	49	16	47	25	■
■						■								■
■		36	37	4	24	31	■	9	26	8	53	1	30	31	■
						■		■						
17	28	35	48	22	31	■	21	7	■	9	5	27	2	30	29	31
■			■			■			■			■			
■	21	13	■	16	6	10	■	56	15	5	■	57	12	31

Leo Tolstoy, *Anna Karenina*

FAMILY RELATIONS

Use the Scriptures listed for your group and the information in the **Scripture Commentary** to create a profile of Jacob's dealings with your assigned character. Be sure to list the "symptoms" of relational problems, your group's "diagnosis" of the real problem, and the biblical "prescription" that helped Jacob overcome the relational problems he experienced.

- **Jacob's relationship with his parents**
  Genesis 25:27, 28; 27:1-29

  Symptoms:

  Diagnosis:

  Prescription:

- **Jacob's relationship with his brother**
  Genesis 25:29-34; 27:30-45; 33:1-17

  Symptoms:

  Diagnosis:

  Prescription:

- **Jacob's relationship with his God**
  Genesis 25:21-34; 32:1-32

  Symptoms:

  Diagnosis:

  Prescription:

THE FOLLOW-THROUGH FACTOR

Jacob struggled with his relationships to his parents and his brother.

Consider the implications of your last Bible study throughout the next week.

Monday
Read Genesis 25:21-26 and Hebrews 10:23, 24.
   What expectations did your parents have for you? How have these expectations caused you to struggle? helped you?

Tuesday
Read Genesis 25:27-34 and Philippians 2:1-4.
   Were you more like Jacob or Esau when you were growing up? If Jacob, list what you can do to make up for taking advantage of others. If Esau, explain how you might have contributed to the problem, then ask God to help you forgive those who took advantage of you.

Wednesday
Read Genesis 27:1-29 and Psalm 103:13-18.
   Why do you think Jacob wanted his father's blessing enough to lie to get it? Would God have kept his promise concerning Jacob (Genesis 25:23) no matter what Isaac had done? List three things you will trust your heavenly Father to do.

Thursday
Read Genesis 27:30-46 and Luke 6:27-36.
   How should Esau have responded to Jacob's deceptive taking of the blessing? What grudges are you holding against family members? Write out what you need to do to forgive and be restored to each family member.

Friday
Read Genesis 32:1-32 and 1 Peter 3:13-16.
   How has your relationship with God been like Jacob's struggle with God? How has it been different? Briefly outline the story of your relationship with God, making sure to honestly tell of the struggles.

Saturday
Read Genesis 33:1-17 and 1 John 3:16-18.
   After Jacob sought God's blessing instead of human blessings, he was able to humble himself before and give presents to his brother. List three family members and what you could do for or give to them as an expression of your love for them.

LESSON 2
Jacob struggled in his marriage.

Lesson Objectives

In the course of this lesson, students will
- ↝ list expectations people bring into marriage.
- ↝ describe how Jacob encountered and handled difficulties in marriage.
- ↝ apply what they learned from Jacob's marital struggles to similar situations today.

LESSON SCRIPTURE
Genesis 29:16–30:24

SCRIPTURE COMMENTARY

It's unlikely that people today will struggle with the same marital situation that Jacob did, but many, if not most, will probably encounter similar difficulties.

Jacob struggled with a lack of romantic love in marriage—Jacob, like most people today, wanted to feel the pleasure of passionate love in his marriage. Unfortunately, Laban's deception complicated Jacob's desire for a marriage based on romantic love.

It seems likely that Jacob loved Rachel rather than Leah because of the former's overall beauty. Leah, on the one hand, had "weak" eyes (whether in brilliance or in vision, we cannot know); Rachel, on the other, was "lovely in form" and beautiful in every way (Genesis 29:17). Because of Rachel's beauty and Jacob's attraction to her, he offered to become Laban's servant for seven years, a generous offer that was not likely to be rejected.

Laban accepted, though without stating in so many words that he would give Jacob Rachel (Genesis 29:19). Likewise, when the seven years were finished, Jacob simply asked for "his wife," not realizing that Laban planned to give him Leah, the firstborn, rather than Rachel (29:21, 23, 26).

At this point Jacob had a decision to make: should he reject unloved Leah, his lawful wife, or finish the week-long ceremony and take Leah fully as his wife? It is to Jacob's credit that he chose the latter course.

Of course, Jacob knew that he would also have Rachel for his wife (Genesis 29:27, 28), but Jacob's decision to accept Leah and to treat her fully as his wife teaches us an important lesson. Jacob sought both passion and commitment in his marriage, but when he found himself, through no fault of his own, in a passionless marriage, he still kept his commitment to his wife. Jacob both finished the week-long ceremony and had children with Leah (an important consideration in that culture) because he was committed to her as his wife. God, for his part, compensated Leah for not being loved and gave her children to increase her status within that culture (29:31-35).

Jacob struggled with infertility in marriage—As Jacob struggled with a lack of romantic love for Leah, he also struggled with the problem of infertility with Rachel. The culture of Jacob's day expected women to bear children and valued them for their ability to bear sons.

Rightly or wrongly, Rachel's inability to become pregnant both disgraced her and created the likelihood that society and her family would devalue her (Genesis 29:31; 30:1). To make matters worse, her sister Leah immediately bore four sons (Genesis 29:31-35) and thus elevated her standing.

Rachel sought to solve her problem in several ways. First, Rachel gave Jacob her servant Bilhah to take as a wife (Genesis 30:3, 4). Rachel would legally bear children for Jacob through this concubine. Later, Rachel bargained with Leah for mandrakes, the small applelike fruit of which was considered an aphrodisiac and an aid to conception. Unfortunately, although Rachel got her mandrakes, Leah got her man, Jacob, and yet another son (30:15-18).

As Jacob recognized from the outset, only God could provide children to Rachel (Genesis 30:2), and, in time, God did give Rachel a son (30:22-24). Jacob worked within the culture of his day to overcome Rachel's struggle with infertility. He agreed to her plan to gain a son through his culture's version of adoption. Still, Jacob also realized that God alone opens and closes wombs, so he trusted God to give Rachel her child in his time and in his way.

Jacob struggled with competition in his marriage—Jacob's polygamous marriage not only created the struggles of a lack of romantic love and infertility, it also led to fierce competition between his wives. Rachel and Leah used children, that culture's symbol of status and security, to compete for their husband's favor.

Leah, for example, expressed a heartfelt hope that Jacob would love her after the birth of her first son (Genesis 29:32). After the birth of a third son, Leah confidently assumed that Jacob would become attached to her, the unloved wife (29:34). Finally, when Leah had born Jacob six sons, she announced that Jacob would treat her with honor (30:20).

Rachel's antagonism toward Leah is even more striking. First, Rachel became jealous of Leah's ability to bear children (Genesis 30:1). To compete with her sister, Rachel legally bore children for Jacob through a concubine. After the birth of a son, Rachel announced that she had been vindicated by God (30:6); following the birth of another son, Rachel declared, "I have had a great struggle with my sister, and I have won" (30:8).

The competition between the two climaxed when Rachel purchased mandrakes from Leah in exchange for one night alone with Jacob. In the midst of this competition, Jacob seems passive, which may be to his credit. According to the rules of that culture, Jacob treated both wives fairly, one might even say equally. Jacob refused to engage in the competition. Rather, he looked out for the interests of both wives even as he trusted God to even the score as he saw fit (see 30:2).

The particulars of Jacob's marital situation are not likely to be duplicated in the lives of your class members, but the struggles that he faced and the truths that his story reveals transcend cultural boundaries. Use this lesson to help your students discover that everyone faces struggles in marriage and that even the most difficult of struggles can, with God's help, be overcome. ✍

Hebrew Helps

The societal stigma of barrenness can be more easily understood when we note that the same Hebrew word, "aqar," is sometimes used in a military sense. When referring to a nation, "aqar" can mean being totally uprooted and destroyed. (See Daniel 7:8 and Zephaniah 2:4, for example.) In other words, a barren woman is symbolic of God conquering a society by literally denying it a future.

All three patriarchs, Abraham, Isaac, and Jacob, had wives described as "barren" (Genesis 11:30; 25:21; 29:31). In each case, Jehovah overcame that barrenness and allowed the nation they were founding to have a future. This hope is echoed when Moses promises that God will not judge his people with barrenness if they are faithful to him (Exodus 23:26; Deuteronomy 7:14).

GETTING A HOLD . . .

Use one of the following activities to help your class list expectations that people bring into marriage.

Materials Needed

↝ newsprint, markers, masking tape

Idealized Portraits

Time: 7-10 minutes

Have people form same-gender groups of five or six. Give each group a sheet of newsprint and several markers.

Explain that each group is to draw a picture, with explanatory comments, of the "perfect mate." For example, groups might sketch and identify a person with loving eyes, a keen mind, strong hands, or feet willing to go the extra mile. Tell groups they have four minutes to create their pictures, after which they will display and explain them to the rest of the class.

After four minutes, have groups take turns presenting their pictures. Then ask the entire class the following questions:

- **How realistic do you think it is to expect to find these perfect mates today?**
- **In your opinion, what are most people looking for when they get married?**
- **What do you think are invalid expectations of marriage? valid expectations?**

Allow adequate time for discussion, then read or summarize in your own words the following transition into the Bible study: **"People often approach marriage with high expectations . . . but most discover early on that it is not all a bed of roses. Every couple struggles with unanticipated difficulties and disappointed expectations. Jacob certainly did. So let's take a look at the marital struggles Jacob experienced and how he overcame those struggles to make his marital life the best that it could be."**

Materials Needed

↝ one photocopy of the "High Expectations" handout from page 21 for each person, paper, pencils, access to a chalkboard and chalk (or newsprint, tape, and a marker)

High Expectations

Time: 10-12 minutes

As class members arrive, hand each person a copy of the handout and a pencil. Explain that participants have four minutes to identify the top five expectations that members of their sex have when they approach marriage. Students should place check marks by the five expectations they think are most typical.

After four minutes, collect the handouts, being sure to keep women's and men's handouts separate. Have people form same-gender groups of four or five. Give each group a sheet of paper. Then challenge group members to write down in order the top five expectations they think the other sex will identify. While groups work, tabulate the results for each group.

When the groups finish their predictions, have the women's groups take turns reporting their "number 1" answers, their "number 2" answers, and so on. After all the women's groups have reported their answers, write the results you tabulated earlier on the chalkboard. Then repeat the process for the men's groups. If you want, award teams ten points for each correct answer and give the winning team a round of applause.

Have students discuss the following questions within their groups. After each question, ask for volunteers to summarize their groups' responses.

- **Which of these expectations are valid? Which are invalid? Why?**
- **How do the situations of life at times disappoint these expectations?**
- **How are marriages affected when these expectations are not met?**
- **How do people generally respond to these disappointed expectations?**

Allow adequate time for discussion, then read or summarize in your own words the following transition into the Bible study: **"People often approach marriage with high expectations . . . but most discover early on that it is not all a bed of roses. Every couple struggles with unanticipated difficulties and disappointed expectations. Jacob certainly did. So let's take a look at the marital struggles Jacob experienced and how he overcame those struggles to make his marital life the best that it could be."**

TAKING IT TO THE MAT . . .

Use one of the following activities to help the class describe how Jacob encountered and handled difficulties in marriage.

Troubleshooting Tips

Time: 18-20 minutes

Before class, make one copy of the "Marriage Troubleshooting Manual" handout and one copy of the **Scripture Commentary** for every four people.

Have people remain in their groups from the opening activity. Tell students they are to work together in their groups to produce a "Marriage Troubleshooting Manual" derived from the life of Jacob. Each group will read an assigned Scripture to identify the marital struggle Jacob faced, then write a brief story that offers a modern example of the same struggle. Finally, group members will create troubleshooting guidelines to help people today either avoid or correct this problem.

Assign each group one of the following passages: Genesis 29:16-35; Genesis 29:31–30:6, 21-24; Genesis 30:1-24. Then give each group a copy of the handout and the **Scripture Commentary,** explaining that groups have ten minutes to create their sections of the manual, after which groups will teach each other what they have learned.

Circulate among groups while they work, commenting as necessary to make sure that the following points are made:

Materials Needed

↝ *Bibles, photocopies of the "Marriage Troubleshooting Manual" handout on page 22, photocopies of the* **Scripture Commentary,** *pencils*

Genesis 29:16-35—*There was a lack of romantic love in Jacob's marriage to Leah, but Jacob still kept his marital commitment to her by keeping her as his wife and by fathering children with her.*

Genesis 29:31–30:6, 21-24—*Infertility plagued Jacob's marriage to Rachel, so Jacob did what he could to give her children through Bilhah and trusted God to give Rachel children in his own time.*

Genesis 30:1-24—*Rachel and Leah used children to compete for Jacob's favor, but Jacob treated both as equals and trusted God to even the score as he saw fit.*

After ten minutes, have groups take turns presenting the information on their handouts. If several groups worked on the same Scripture, invite them to present different parts of the manual.

Then invite people to silently think about the following questions. Allow thirty seconds of reflection time after each question.

- **In what ways is your situation different from Jacob's? How is it similar?**
- **Which of the troubleshooting tips do you need to apply to your life today?**

Lead into the next section of the lesson by reading or restating the following in your own words: **"It's doubtful that any of us will be in the same kind of situation that Jacob faced, but many of us will still experience the kind of struggles that Jacob encountered. Whether it's a lack of romantic love, the pain of infertility, or even a problem with competition between spouses—we will all probably face at some time or another the struggle of a marriage that's not all that it was supposed to be. So let's spend a few minutes discussing how we can apply the troubleshooting tips learned from Jacob's marital struggles to our own situations today."**

Marital Roles

Time: 15-18 minutes

Have class members form three groups. If your class is large, have people form six groups. Assign each group one of the following Scripture passages: Genesis 29:16-35; Genesis 29:31–30:6, 21-24; Genesis 30:1-24. Give each group paper, pens, and a copy of the **Scripture Commentary.**

Explain that group members are to read their passage and the relevant section of the **Scripture Commentary** to discover the marital struggle that Jacob faced and how Jacob dealt with that struggle. Then group members are to brainstorm a two-minute role play that depicts the same marital struggle (but not its resolution) today. Groups have five minutes to create the role plays. Then they will present their mini-dramas and explain how Jacob would have dealt with that situation. Encourage every group member to be involved, either in writing the role play, performing it, or explaining after the role play how Jacob dealt with the situation.

If needed, use the following ideas to help groups get started with their role plays.

Materials Needed

↝ Bibles, photocopies of the **Scripture Commentary,** pens, paper

Genesis 29:16-35—*Tom and Joan married after a long courtship, mainly because everyone expected them to. Unfortunately, their feelings for each other were always rather cool. To make matters worse, recently Tom has been paying special attention to Shelley, Joan's best friend. In short, Tom's loyalty still remains with Joan, but his heart is being tugged toward Shelley.*

Genesis 29:31–30:6, 21-24—*For years Mike and Dana have focused on their careers to the exclusion of nearly everything else. Recently, however, they've been thinking and talking about starting a family. Unfortunately, they have had little success with that, and now their fertility specialist says that their chances of having kids of their own are practically nil.*

Genesis 30:1-24—*Jack and Diane were both raised in large families, and both had to fight for their rights while growing up. The only problem is that they've carried that attitude into their marriage. If Diane gets a promotion, Jack works even harder, spending longer hours to try and match her accomplishment. When they are with friends, Jack and Diane try to point out the other's mistakes and take special pains to show their own superiority over the other.*

After five minutes, invite groups to present their role plays and to explain how Jacob would have dealt with this struggle. Then invite people to silently think about the following questions. Allow thirty seconds of reflection time after each question.

- **Which of these struggles is most similar to your current marital situation?**
- **How might you follow Jacob's example to avoid or to correct this struggle?**

Lead into the next section of the lesson by reading or restating the following in your own words: **"It's doubtful that any of us will be in the same kind of situation that Jacob faced, but many of us will still experience the kind of struggles that Jacob encountered. Whether it's a lack of romantic love, the pain of infertility, or even a problem with competition between spouses—we will all probably face at some time or another the struggle of a marriage that's not all that it was supposed to be. So let's spend a few minutes discussing how we can apply the lessons learned from Jacob's marital struggles to our own situations today."**

PINNING IT DOWN . . .

Use one or both of the following activities to help class members apply what they learned from Jacob's marital struggles to similar situations today.

Modern Problems

Time: 12-15 minutes

Remind learners that most people approach marriage with certain expectations such as romance, children, and an equal partnership but that many couples struggle

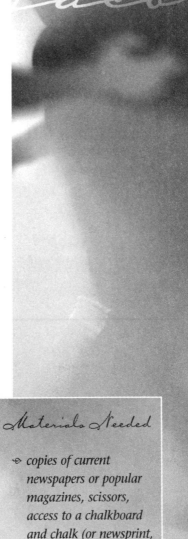

Materials Needed

↦ *copies of current newspapers or popular magazines, scissors, access to a chalkboard and chalk (or newsprint, tape, and a marker)*

with difficulties such as a lack of romantic love, infertility, or competition between spouses. Write the difficulties on the chalkboard or newsprint.

Ask students to call out other difficulties with which modern couples struggle. Write people's ideas on the chalkboard or newsprint. After listing four or five ideas, have learners form groups of four or five. Give each group several newspapers or magazines and scissors.

Explain that group members are to cut out articles or pictures that offer real-life examples of the marital struggles listed. While groups work, circulate among them offering suggestions and guidance.

Allow five minutes for research, then ask for groups to report what they found. After each example, ask the entire class how people often react in that situation and how they might apply the lessons they learned in the Bible study to that struggle.

Close by reading or restating the following in your own words: **"Like Jacob, each one of us will probably struggle with certain aspects of marriage. Perhaps you want, but cannot seem to enjoy, romantic love for your partner. Or maybe you and your spouse feel the pain of infertility. Perhaps you even experience marital competition rather than mutual cooperation in your marriage. Whatever your struggle, you can improve your relationship by applying the lessons seen in the life of Jacob, by taking whatever steps you can to overcome that struggle and by trusting God to honor your commitment to your marriage and your spouse."**

Then move on to the next section or close the lesson in prayer.

The Follow-Through Factor

Time: 5 minutes

This section appears in every lesson in this series. This weekly devotion plan helps class members apply the Bible study throughout the coming week. You may use it immediately after the Bible study or in conjunction with the preceding activity.

Give each person a copy of the handout. Take time to briefly read through it, but do not discuss any of the questions at this time.

Close the session in prayer

Materials Needed

⤷ one copy of "The Follow-Through Factor" handout from page 23 for each person

HIGH EXPECTATIONS

Read through the following list of expectations and place check marks by the five most common expectations that members of your gender have as they approach marriage. Then indicate at the bottom whether you are male or female.

_____ companionship

_____ children

_____ romantic love

_____ relational equality

_____ emotional support

_____ complete acceptance

_____ room for personal growth

_____ financial support

_____ someone to have fun with

_____ sexual intimacy

_____ personal freedom

_____ financial stability

_____ lifetime commitment

_____ "happily ever after"

_____ personal intimacy

_____ individual worth

_____ someone to keep house

_____ a nurturing family unit

_____ **Male** _____ **Female**

MARRIAGE TROUBLESHOOTING MANUAL

Read through your assigned Scripture in order to discover the particular nature of Jacob's marital struggle. Then write a short story of a modern example of the same struggle. Finally, list several principles to help people either avoid (preventative) or properly deal with (corrective) this struggle today.

Jacob's struggle:

A modern parallel:

Troubleshooting tips:

Preventative measures:

Corrective measures:

THE FOLLOW-THROUGH FACTOR

Jacob struggled in his marriage.

Consider the implications of your last Bible study throughout the next week.

Monday
Read Genesis 29:16-20 and Song of Solomon 8:6, 7.
Why do you think Jacob loved Rachel but not Leah? Why do you think God created humans with the capacity to feel passionate love? What do you think is the place of romantic love in marriage?

Tuesday
Read Genesis 29:21-30 and Proverbs 5:15-23.
How did Jacob keep his marital commitment to Leah? Why do you think Jacob kept his commitment even though he didn't love Leah? Write what you can do to better keep your commitments in the areas of marriage, family, or your relationship with God.

Wednesday
Read Genesis 29:31-35 and Matthew 5:3-12.
List below two disappointments in marriage or life that trouble you. Then list two to three ways God has compensated you for each disappointment.

Thursday
Read Genesis 30:1, 2 and Psalm 127.
Why do you think children are considered such a blessing from God? Why might God decide not to give children to some couples? How might God compensate for the lack of children in a marriage?

Friday
Read Genesis 30:3-21 and Philippians 3:12-14.
How did Rachel and Leah's competition disrupt their family life? For what do you compete? How does your striving for superiority affect your family life? your relationship with God?

Saturday
Read Genesis 30:22-24 and Psalm 34:4-7.
God takes away the disgrace of those who seek him. How has he taken away shame in your life? Whom can you tell about God's merciful deliverance from shame? Write what you will say to this person so he or she can become a child of God too.

LESSON 3

Jacob struggled in his business relationships.

LESSON SCRIPTURE

Genesis 30:25–31:55

SCRIPTURE COMMENTARY

Everyone faces struggles at work. Consequently, everyone can benefit from the lessons learned from Jacob's experiences in his business life.

Jacob struggled to earn enough to provide for his family—After fourteen years of hard labor and faithful service, Jacob had little to show for his efforts. Granted, Jacob had added wives and children to his household, but even his family members still remained under his father-in-law's control (Genesis 30:26). Moreover, Jacob owned no personal goods that he could leave to his family when he died. So Jacob decided that enough was enough: it was time to look for greener pastures (30:25).

Laban, recognizing that his increase in wealth was due to God's blessing of Jacob, desperately wanted Jacob to stay (30:27). Laban even offered to *give* Jacob whatever wages he named if he would simply agree to continue in Laban's service (30:31).

Jacob, however, did not want Laban's gifts (30:31). Jacob trusted God to honor his efforts and to give him a fair wage for his labors. So Jacob proposed that Laban allow him to take any dark-colored lambs, speckled or spotted sheep, or speckled or spotted goats from Laban's herds and to place them in his own (30:32). If Laban would agree to this, Jacob would continue to care for both Laban's and his own flocks (30:31, 33).

Jacob's proposal, though possibly odd at first glance, was an expression of faith in God. The goats of that region were generally dark brown or black, while sheep were usually white. In other words, multicolored sheep or goats and dark-colored lambs were exceptional and not a promising resource for building a large herd. But Jacob, presumably recognizing that God had been blessing him all along (30:30), offered to take these animals as his wages. Jacob did not want Laban's gifts, which would have obligated him even more to Laban. Rather, Jacob demanded that Laban pay him and then trusted God to bless his faithful labors.

Jacob struggled when treated unethically by his boss—Jacob's agreement to work for a specified wage (Genesis 30:31-33) should have ended his struggles with Laban, but such was not to be the case.

The very same day that Laban had agreed to give Jacob all the speckled or spotted sheep, speckled or spotted goats, and dark-colored lambs, he secretly removed some of these animals so Jacob could not find them (30:35, 36). What was Jacob to do?

First, one should note that Jacob did not retaliate by "grasping" (as was his habit) what rightfully belonged to him. In fact, it appears that Jacob did not even confront Laban for this theft. Rather, Jacob worked within his job description as keeper of the flocks and used the cultural practices of his day to thwart Laban's unethical dealings.

Shepherds of Jacob's time believed that what an animal saw while mating would affect the offspring conceived at that moment. So Jacob placed striped pieces of wood in front of mating animals to cause them to bear striped, streaked, or spotted young (30:37-39). Jacob also practiced selective breeding. That is, he placed the branches in front of the stronger females when they mated but not in view of the weaker ones. In this way Jacob built up a large herd of strong, multicolored sheep and goats (30:41, 42). In time Jacob parleyed his initial holdings into a vast household that contained large flocks, servants, camels, and donkeys (30:43).

In sum, Jacob overcame Laban's unethical actions by refusing to seize what was legitimately his and by trusting God to honor his efforts to work with integrity and with intelligence (31:11, 12).

Jacob struggled in a hostile work environment—God had blessed Jacob's labors (see Genesis 30:43), but this did not mean that Jacob enjoyed his work situation. In fact, Jacob struggled so much with his boss (Laban) and his co-workers (Laban's sons) that eventually he felt compelled to leave.

Laban's earlier attitude toward Jacob (30:27, 28) had taken a marked turn for the worse (31:2, 5), and Laban's sons resented Jacob's prosperity because it came at their father's (and presumably their own) expense (31:1). To make matters worse, Laban had repeatedly changed Jacob's wages even after the two had agreed on Jacob's pay (31:6-8, 41; 30:34). All signs indicated that it was time for Jacob to leave.

As is often the case, Jacob's outward circumstances were confirmed by an inner voice, by the voice of God telling Jacob to return to his own family back in Canaan (31:3, 13). But this would be no easy departure.

First, Jacob left without telling Laban that he was going (31:20, 21). In addition, Rachel took her father's household gods (possibly tokens of inheritance) without telling anyone that she had done so (31:19, 32). When Laban discovered both the flight and the theft, he gathered his forces and pursued Jacob and his family (31:22, 23, 30).

Had God not warned Laban against harming Jacob (31:24), it might have been a deadly meeting. As it was, Laban was unable to prove the charge of theft (31:33-35) and unable to rebut Jacob's claim to loyal service (31:36-42), so he proposed that he and Jacob end their relationship with an agreement to prevent future problems or misunderstandings (31:43-54).

Struggles at work are both inevitable and insidious, threatening people's bank accounts and dominating their personal lives. But even the worst of problems can be overcome if people apply the principles revealed in the life of Jacob to their own unique situations today. ✎

Hebrew Helps

The modern reader may become uneasy when learning that Laban discovered Jacob's value to him "by divination" (30:27). The Hebrew word, "nachash," is actually an onomatopoeia, a word that is defined by the sound it makes (such as the English words, "drip," "pop," and "zip"). When pronounced it suggests a "hiss" or a "whisper," such as the sound of a sorcerer making an incantation. In a noun form, the same word is translated over thirty times in the Old Testament as "serpent" (Genesis 3:1, 2, 4), for even more obvious reasons.

While the verb is usually translated as having to do with "divination" (Genesis 44:5; Leviticus 19:26; 2 Chronicles 33:6), it is also used idiomatically to mean to take "as a good sign" (1 Kings 20:33).

Whether Laban learned of Jacob's value by pagan practices or by shrewd observation ("by experience," KJV), he did not act wisely upon his knowledge. Knowledge from any source, used without moral judgment, can lead one astray.

GETTING A HOLD . . .

Use one of the following activities to help people recognize that no one is immune from difficulties while at work.

Materials Needed

↦ four or five work-related prizes such as PayDay® candy bars or coffee cups with work-related themes

Work Woes

Time: 7-10 minutes

Inform class members that you are going to start class by holding a storytelling contest. Have people form groups of four or five. People have one minute each to tell their group members about the worst job they've ever had. After each person has told a story, group members are to choose what they think is the worst job told about in the group.

Remind class members that their stories don't have to tell about their experiences at paid positions. Their worst jobs may relate to chores they had growing up, work they have done around the house, or even volunteer work they have performed.

When all the groups have selected their "worst" stories, have the people whose stories were selected take turns recounting their terrible jobs. Then have the entire class select what they think is the worst job described by the storytellers. Reward all the members of the winning group with the work-related prizes.

Then ask the entire class to discuss the following questions:

- **Was it easy or difficult for you to think of a truly bad job?**
- **What do you think this says about our work experiences?**
- **What did all of our worst-job stories have in common?**
- **What do you consider to be the elements of a good job?**
- **What types of problems or situations might make a job bad?**

Then read or summarize in your own words the following transition into the Bible study: **"It doesn't matter whether you work at home or in a paid position—you have probably had to face and endure some sort of work-related problem. There's no need to feel bad if you have. Even Jacob struggled in his business relationships. Let's spend some time examining God's Word to learn what types of struggles Jacob faced in his work and to discover how he overcame those work-related struggles."**

Materials Needed

↦ photocopies of the "Job Search" puzzle from page 31, pencils

Job Search

Time: 10-12 minutes

As people arrive, hand each person a copy of the puzzle and a pencil. The puzzle contains two lists of words. One describes things that make work good or enjoyable, while the other describes problems or situations that make work difficult. People are to find the words hidden in the puzzle to complete both lists.

The positive words hidden in the puzzle are: *achievement, approval, paycheck, promotion, relationships, security,* and *teamwork.* The puzzle's negative words are: *corruption, criticism, dishonesty, exploitation, failure, favoritism,* and *hostility.*

After everyone has arrived and most have found a good number of words, ask people to call out the words they found. Then have people form groups of four to discuss the following questions. Allow a minute for discussion after each question, then ask for volunteers to report their groups' answers.

- **How many of these negative aspects have you faced in your own work?**
- **What do you think this reveals about people's typical work experiences?**
- **How did encountering these problems affect your attitude toward work?**
- **How did you respond when you encountered these situations at work?**

Then read or summarize in your own words the following transition into the Bible study: **"It doesn't matter whether you work at home or in a paid position—you have probably had to face and endure some sort of work-related problem. There's no need to feel bad if you have. Even Jacob struggled in his business relationships. Let's spend some time examining God's Word to learn what types of struggles Jacob faced in his work and to discover how he overcame those work-related struggles."**

```
    D I S H O N E S T Y   S
A     K R O W M A E T P
C R I T I C I S M   I A E
H             H R Y X
I E R U L I A F S   U C P
E N       N     C H L
V   O     O     E E O
E Y T I L I T S O H S C I
M       T     K T
E   F A V O R I T I S M A
N   L     M       T
T E     O       I
R   N O I T P U R R O C O
    L A V O R P P A   N
```

TAKING IT TO THE MAT . . .

Use one of the following activities to help learners discover how Jacob encountered and handled difficulties in his business.

Job Interviews

Time: 15-18 minutes

Have class members form three groups. Assign each group one of the following passages: Genesis 30:25-33; Genesis 30:34-43 and 31:10-12; Genesis 31:1-9, 13-55. Give each group paper, pencils, and a copy of the **Scripture Commentary.**

Explain that group members are to read the assigned Scripture and then prepare interview questions with Jacob about his job situation. Their questions should

Materials Needed

↪ *Bibles, photocopies of* **the Scripture Commentary,** *pencils, paper*

help other members of the class understand what struggle Jacob faced in the passage, how Jacob responded to this struggle, and why Jacob reacted as he did. Groups have eight minutes to create their interviews.

If you prefer not to use an "interview" format, use the suggested questions to guide learners' study of the assigned passages. Students can present their answers to these research questions to the rest of the class.

As people work, circulate from group to group answering questions and guiding discussion. If needed, offer some of the following questions as samples.

Genesis 30:25-33—*What was your motivation for wanting to leave Laban? Why did you ask if you could take your wives and children?*

Why did you refuse Laban's offer of a gift? What do you think Laban's reason for making this offer might have been?

Your offer to take the differently colored goats and sheep seems a bit odd. What was the thinking behind this proposal?

Genesis 30:34-43; 31:10-12—*Laban was wrong to take the animals he had pledged to you. Why didn't you just seize what was rightfully yours?*

Placing striped branches in front of mating animals seems bizarre. How did you come up with this odd but effective idea?

How do you explain your rapid increase in wealth, going from abject poverty to astounding prosperity in such a short time?

Genesis 31:1-9, 13-55—*After being with Laban for twenty years, what led to your final decision to leave his employment and his presence?*

Why did you leave in secret, without telling Laban that you were going? Do you think this was the wisest course of action?

Why did you eventually agree to make a covenant with Laban? What did you hope to accomplish with this covenant?

After eight minutes, have groups briefly summarize the events of their passages and then role-play the interviews with Jacob. Supplement the interviews as needed to ensure that students understand that:

1. **Jacob didn't seek a gift from Laban. He wanted to earn what he deserved because he trusted God to bless him.**

2. **Jacob did not retaliate for Laban's theft by seizing what was his. Instead, he worked within his job description to gain his rightful wages even as he trusted God to give him his due.**

3. **Jacob left because it wasn't going to get any better and God told him it was time to leave. He made a covenant with Laban to avoid future misunderstandings.**

Then lead into the next section by reading or restating the following in your own words: **"Struggles in our work are probably unavoidable, but we can honor God and overcome these struggles by applying the lessons revealed through the life of Jacob. Like Jacob, we need to work for what we need, maintain integrity even when those around us don't, and trust God to** prosper us in that situation or tell us that it's time to move on. So let's close today's study by committing ourselves to following Jacob's example in our own work situations."

Cases to Consider

Time: 18-20 minutes

Keep people in their groups from the opening activity. Give each group a copy of the "Cases to Consider" handout, a copy of the **Scripture Commentary,** and a pencil. Assign each group one of the following passages: **Genesis 30:25-33; Genesis 30:34-43; and Genesis 31:1-55.**

Explain that group members are to read their Scripture passage and the relevant section of the **Scripture Commentary** to identify the nature of Jacob's work struggle and how he responded to that struggle. Then group members are to read their case study and discuss how Jacob would handle this situation. After ten minutes, groups will report their discoveries to the rest of the class.

Move from group to group as students work, offering suggestions to help people discover the following points and possible solutions to the case studies.

Genesis 30:25-33—*Jacob didn't seek a gift from Laban. Rather, he wanted to earn what he deserved because he trusted God to bless him. (Jack might reject the bonus and offer to work on commission instead, trusting God to bless his efforts.)*

Genesis 30:34-43—*Jacob didn't retaliate for Laban's theft by seizing what was his. Instead, he worked within his job description to gain his rightful wages even as he trusted God to give him his due. (Lois could establish another account to hold her legitimate share of the profits, then trust God to reward her as he sees fit during the last six months of her work year.)*

Genesis 31:1-55—*Jacob left because it wasn't going to get any better and God told him it was time to leave. In the end, he made a covenant with Laban to avoid any future misunderstandings. (Dave might decide that the best solution would be for him to leave. He could explain to his boss and co-workers his reasons for leaving and make sure that his relationships with them were as good as they could be.)*

After ten minutes, have groups take turns briefly summarizing Jacob's struggle and solution, reading the case studies, and explaining how Jacob would respond in this situation. Invite other groups to offer their ideas on how Jacob might react.

Then lead into the next section by reading or restating the following in your own words: **"Struggles in our work are probably unavoidable, but we can honor God and overcome these struggles by applying the lessons revealed through the life of Jacob. Like Jacob, we need to work for what we need, maintain integrity even when those around us don't, and trust God to prosper us in that situation or tell us that it's time to move on. So let's close today's study by committing ourselves to following Jacob's example in our own work situations."**

Materials Needed

⇥ *Bibles, photocopies of the "Cases to Consider" handout from page 32, photocopies of the* **Scripture Commentary,** *pencils*

PINNING IT DOWN . . .

Use one or both of the following activities to help learners commit to applying the lessons revealed in the life of Jacob to their own work situations.

Materials Needed

✎ newsprint, a marker, tape, play money (preferably $100 bills), pens

The Buck Stops Here

Time: 12-15 minutes

Before class, write the following phrases on the sheet of newsprint: **inadequate wages, unethical employer, hostile work environment.**

Begin by hanging the sheet of newsprint where everyone can see it. Invite class members to describe several modern examples for each area of struggle. After each area has several examples, write the principles learned from the life of Jacob under each heading. Then ask people to describe how Jacob would respond to at least one modern problem listed in each area. Invite learners to suggest other biblical truths that could be applied to the situations.

After several minutes of discussion, hold up a $100 bill and remind people that work struggles—whether one works at home or on the job—are scary because they always involve money. People struggle to make enough to survive, have what is rightfully theirs taken by unethical people, or face potential loss of income because of intolerable situations.

Then give each person a $100 bill and a pen. Have everyone choose one area of struggle listed on the newsprint with which he or she closely relates. Allow people time to think, then have them write the principle for that area on the backs of their $100 bills.

When everyone has written a principle, have students form groups with those who chose the same area. Ask group members to briefly share their work concerns, to discuss how they could apply the principle to each situation, and to pray for each group member, asking God to guide and bless that person in his or her work situation.

Then move on to the next section or close the lesson by encouraging students to take their $100 bill bookmarks home as a reminder of the lesson they learned today.

Materials Needed

✎ one copy of "The Follow-Through Factor" handout from page 33 for each person

The Follow-Through Factor

Time: 5 minutes

This section appears in every lesson in this series. This weekly devotion plan helps class members apply the Bible study throughout the coming week. You may use it immediately after the Bible study or in conjunction with the preceding activity.

Give each person a copy of the handout. Take time to briefly read through it, but do not discuss any of the questions at this time.

Close the session in prayer.

JOB SEARCH

Contained within the word-search puzzle below are fourteen words: seven describe positive aspects of work, and seven describe problems or situations that make work difficult. When you find a word, circle it and write it on the appropriate blank line.

```
E D I S H O N E S T Y A S
A I C K R O W M A E T P C
C R I T I C I S M N I A E
H P A R J X O D F H R Y X
I E R U L I A F S G U C P
E N H O Z K W N L U C H L
V M O N T R O Q U V E E O
E Y T I L I T S O H S C I
M A U Q T C T D O O S K T
E M F A V O R I T I S M A
N O L S F T M I N G R I T
T E L E M O R O J G V H I
R U N O I T P U R R O C O
T R A L A V O R P P A Y N
```

Positive   **Negative**

_____   _____

_____   _____

_____   _____

_____   _____

_____   _____

_____   _____

_____   _____

CASES TO CONSIDER

Read your assigned Scripture and the information in the **Scripture Commentary** to discover what work-related struggle Jacob faced and how he overcame that struggle. Then read your assigned case study below and discuss how Jacob might handle this situation today.

Living From Hand to Mouth
Genesis 30:25-33

Jack has worked at the same salaried sales position for fourteen years. He enjoys the challenge of his job and the people he works with, but he barely ekes out enough to support his wife and five children. At the end of his financial rope, Jack informs his boss that he intends to look for another job that will allow him to buy a house and build for the future. Jack's employer knows that much of her success is due to Jack, so she offers to give him a bonus worth one month's salary if he will agree to stay. How could Jack apply Jacob's example in this situation?

Robbing the Till
Genesis 30:34-43

When Lois signed on as the business manager of a software development firm, her employer agreed to set aside 2 percent of each month's profits into a special account, which Lois would receive as a profit-sharing bonus after her one-year anniversary. Just prior to her six-month review, however, Lois discovered that her employer had transferred funds from this account into his own personal savings account. What do you think Jacob would do in this situation?

Hostility All Around
Genesis 31:1-55

Dave, a construction supervisor, has gotten great reviews each of the three years he has worked for his current contractor. Recently, however, he has noticed a change in attitude in both his employer and the people he supervises. His boss seems to resent the amount of money that Dave earns, while his co-workers think that they deserve to be paid as much as Dave is. Both Dave's boss and his co-workers have made work completely miserable for Dave, spreading lies about his personal life and criticizing his every decision. How could Dave follow Jacob's example in this situation?

©1999 by The Standard Publishing Company. Permission is granted to reproduce this page for ministry purposes only—not for resale.

THE FOLLOW-THROUGH FACTOR

Jacob struggled in his business relationships.

Consider the implications of your last Bible study throughout the next week.

Monday
Read Genesis 30:25-33 and 12:1-3.
   Like his grandfather Abram, Jacob was a channel through whom God blessed others. Who are two people whom God could bless through your work? What do you need to do to become a channel of divine blessing to them?

Tuesday
Read Genesis 30:34-43 and Matthew 10:16.
   In what ways was Jacob as shrewd as a snake? as innocent as a dove? Which of these two animals are you most like at work? How can you strike a better balance between the two? Ask God to help you work with intelligence and integrity.

Wednesday
Read Genesis 31:1-13 and Acts 15:36-41.
   Why do you think God instructed Jacob to leave Laban? What relationships in your own life might God want you to end? How can you show love to those whom God might ask you to leave behind?

Thursday
Read Genesis 31:14-30 and 2 Corinthians 12:1-10.
   Laban had all the earthly power in this situation, but Jacob possessed divine power and protection. What is one situation in which you feel like Jacob, with little or no earthly power?

Friday
Read Genesis 31:31-42 and Proverbs 3:27-30.
   To what extent do you think Jacob's accusation against Laban (v. 42) was true? Who may have taken advantage of you? How should you respond to that person? Whom have you taken advantage of? How can you make it right with that person?

Saturday
Read Genesis 31:43-55 and Matthew 5:25, 26.
   How did this covenant provide a good ending to Jacob and Laban's quarrels? With whom do you need to follow their example: someone at work? a friend? a family member? a neighbor?

LESSON 4

Jacob struggled in his relationships with his children.

Lesson Objectives

In the course of this lesson, students will

- ✤ discuss dreams parents have for their children.
- ✤ describe how Jacob encountered and handled difficulties with his children.
- ✤ apply the truths of this lesson to modern struggles similar to Jacob's.

LESSON SCRIPTURE

Genesis 34:1-31; 37:2-11; 49:1-28

SCRIPTURE COMMENTARY

Of all the struggles that Jacob faced in his life, that with his children was, in many ways, most disappointing. Still, we can discover valuable truths from Jacob's experiences and thus avoid the struggles that he faced.

Jacob struggled with his children's behavior—One cause of Jacob's problems with his children was his parental inactivity. Nowhere can this be seen more clearly than in Genesis 34:1-31.

At first glance, one might think that Genesis 34 merely recounts a tragic instance of rape (v. 2) and murderous revenge (v. 25). The story does contain those elements, to be sure, but it also contains much more.

In the first place, Shechem committed a heinous crime by raping Dinah, a crime that begged for a just response. Unfortunately, neither Jacob nor his sons responded to Shechem's crime in an appropriate or acceptable manner. Two of Jacob's sons, on the one hand, deceitfully used an act of religious piety (circumcision) to disable and destroy everyone associated with Shechem (34:13-25). To make matters worse, some of Jacob's other sons plundered the town, profiting themselves financially through an attack on their sister (vv. 27-29). It isn't surprising, then, to hear Jacob rebuke his murderous sons for their treacherous deed (v. 30).

This does not mean, however, that Jacob stands without fault. Jacob's sons acted rashly (and wrongly) to avenge their sister as they did, but Jacob erred just as much by failing to act at all. For example, Jacob did nothing other than wait for his sons to get home when he heard what had happened to Dinah (34:5). Then, when Hamor, Shechem's father, approached Jacob with a marriage offer, Jacob sat idly by, letting his sons conduct the tense negotiations (vv. 7-10, 13-17). Whatever Jacob's reasons for failing to demand justice—perhaps he hoped to gain status and wealth through the arrangement (vv. 9, 10, 12)—his inactivity caused far more trouble than he had ever imagined. Jacob's passive parenting style set the stage for his sons' misconduct and his own eventual shame and fears (v. 30).

Jacob struggled with sibling rivalry among his children—Just as Jacob and Esau struggled for supremacy in their family (see Genesis 25:23-34; 27:1-41), so too Jacob's sons fought to gain the upper hand in theirs. Jacob added to this sibling rivalry both by actively favoring one son, Joseph, over the others and by passively allowing it to fester into a raging feud.

For example, Genesis 37:3 reports that Jacob loved Joseph more than any of his other sons. This paternal preference is understandable, since Joseph had been born to Jacob late in life, but Jacob created an explosive situation by publicly showing his favoritism for Joseph, by giving Joseph a special robe. (See sidebar.) It comes as little surprise, then, that Joseph, who had earlier helped tend Jacob's flocks (37:2), now assumed a more elevated role. Joseph spent most of his days at home, leaving only to check on his working brothers so he could report back to Jacob on their condition (vv. 12-14). Because Joseph had already delivered a negative report about four of his brothers (v. 2), conditions were ripe for a serious, potentially deadly, conflict (vv. 17b-32).

To make matters worse, Jacob had earlier permitted Joseph's divinely ordained preeminence to deepen his brothers' antagonism toward him (37:5-11). By neither cautioning Joseph to be discreet about his dreams nor challenging his other sons to accept God's will, Jacob created the conditions in which sibling rivalry would erupt into out-and-out conflict.

Jacob struggled with his children's future—Because Jacob did not deal with his children's behavioral and relational problems when and as he should have, he eventually struggled with and worried about their future. Jacob recognized that the seeds he had planted during their younger days would inevitably grow and flower, some for good and some for evil.

Genesis 49:1-28, which records Jacob's deathbed blessing on his sons, sets out in poetic language what the future would hold for each son. In every case this future reflected the character traits his sons had developed and demonstrated in the past.

Simeon and Levi, for example, earned their father's curse (49:7). Their violent murder of all the men allied with Shechem (34:25, 26) would come back to haunt them and their descendants. These two brothers who lived by the sword would be scattered by the sword for generations to come. In a similar way, Reuben, who had dishonored his father by having sexual relations with Bilhah (35:22), would forfeit the honor due him as Jacob's firstborn son (49:3, 4).

Judah, however, was destined to rule. Earlier Judah had convinced his brothers to spare Joseph's life (37:26, 27). In the future Judah would exercise the same type of leadership over all the sons and tribes of Israel (49:8-12). Likewise, Joseph, who had courageously faced and overcome every obstacle placed in his way (37:17b-36; 39:1–41:57), would continue to prosper and flourish in the days and years to come (49:22-26).

As long as there are children, there will be struggles with children. But those struggles need not destroy families, as they did Jacob's, for God has graciously revealed through the example of Jacob how parents can lovingly and firmly guide their children to a future that will honor God and bring joy to themselves. ✎

The definition of the word describing the robe of Joseph, "passim," is unclear. The singular form of this plural noun is found in Daniel 5. It refers to the "end" of the hand which wrote on the wall of King Belshazzar's banquet room (Daniel 5:5, 24). Some speculate that the coat was made of "ends" or "parts" of many fabrics, therefore, multicolored. Others assume that it refers to a coat that reached the "ends" or "extremities" of the wearer's body, and was therefore, long-sleeved.

The only other use of "passim" in the Old Testament refers to a robe worn by King David's daughter, Tamar. In that passage it is made clear that "this was the kind of garment the virgin daughters of the king wore" (2 Samuel 13:18, 19).

Though the exact nature of Joseph's robe is uncertain, it signified Joseph's exaltation over his brothers. In giving this robe, Jacob was probably indicating that Joseph had been given the "birthright" over his older brothers, as Jacob had been honored over Esau. Is it any wonder that similar hostility existed?

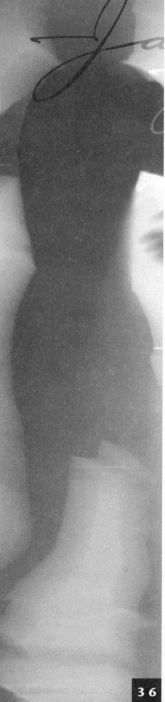

GETTING A HOLD . . .

Use one of the following activities to prompt people to think about various dreams that parents have for their children.

Acrostic Aspirations

Time: 10-12 minutes

As students arrive, give each person a copy of the "Acrostic Aspirations" puzzle and a pencil. Have people read the directions at the top of the handout, then solve the clues to complete the acrostic and discover to whom these aspirations and dreams apply.

When people fill in the following answers to the clues, they will spell the word "children."

C *ash*

H *ealth*

I *ndependence*

L *ove*

D *ependents*

R *esponsibility*

E *mpathy*

N *ormalcy*

When everyone has arrived and most have had a chance to solve the puzzle, ask people to read their answers. If necessary, supply needed answers and announce the word that the puzzle reveals.

Be careful not to assume that everyone in your class is a parent. Some people may have chosen not to have kids, while others might be struggling with infertility. Be sure to include everyone by referring to students' own children as well as children they care about.

Then instruct people to form groups of four and discuss the following questions. Allow several minutes for discussion after each question, then ask for volunteers to report their groups' answers.

- **If a child could attain only four of these, which would you choose? Why?**
- **What other hopes and dreams would you want a child you love to attain?**
- **What do you think keeps children from attaining these dreams as adults?**

Then read or restate in your own words the following transition into the Bible study: **"Few things in life are so filled with promise and fraught with peril as raising children. Parents hope for the best, fear the worst, and struggle to do all that they can to ensure that their kids grow up to be adults who bring honor to their family and to their God. The Bible teaches us many principles for raising children. It also gives us concrete examples of what can happen when these principles aren't applied as**

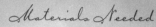

Materials Needed

↝ *pencils, one photocopy of the "Acrostic Aspirations" handout from page 41 for each person*

they should be. Today we'll look at one such example as we investigate Jacob's struggles in his relationships with his children."

When I Grow Up

Time: 7-10 minutes

Materials Needed

↦ *paper, markers*

As people arrive, give each person a sheet of paper and a marker. Instruct people to draw pictures of what, when they were young, they wanted to grow up to be. Tell people to keep what they're drawing secret. Others will try to guess who drew which picture.

After everyone has arrived and had a chance to draw a picture, ask people to give their pictures to you, again without letting anyone see what they drew. Shuffle the pictures, then hold them up one at a time so people can try to guess who drew each picture. If necessary, explain what the pictures depict. If class members cannot guess who drew the picture, ask the artist to identify himself or herself.

When all the artists have been identified, ask class members how many of them actually realized their childhood dreams. Then ask those who did not achieve those dreams why they didn't. After several students share their experiences, ask the entire class the following questions:

* **What future hopes or dreams would you have for a child you love?**
* **What do you think keeps kids from attaining these dreams as adults?**

Then read or restate in your own words the following transition into the Bible study: **"Few things in life are so filled with promise and fraught with peril as raising children. Parents hope for the best, fear the worst, and struggle to do all that they can to ensure that their kids grow up to be adults who bring honor to their family and to their God. The Bible teaches us many principles for raising children. It also gives us concrete examples of what can happen when these principles aren't applied as they should be. Today we'll look at one such example as we investigate Jacob's struggles in his relationships with his children."**

TAKING IT TO THE MAT . . .

Use one of the following activities to help learners describe how Jacob encountered and handled difficulties with his children.

Turning Points

Time: 18-20 minutes

Materials Needed

↦ *Bibles, pencils, paper*

Have learners form groups of four or five, making sure to include both parents and people without children in each group. Assign half the groups Genesis 34:1-31 and the other half Genesis 37:2-36.

Remind students that they can learn from both the Bible's positive and negative examples, then explain that they are to study their assigned passages to identify one or more "turning points" in the story that led to Jacob's struggles with his children. Every time they discover a turning point, they are to identify what Jacob did wrong and discuss what he could have done to avoid the problem that his actions created. (If you prefer, have group members create short skits to portray the biblical stories as well as their new endings.)

Once groups have discussed the turning points, they are to write new endings to the stories to describe what might have happened if Jacob had followed their advice. Groups have ten minutes to finish their rewrites of the stories.

Move from group to group while people work, answering questions and offering suggestions to ensure that the following points are covered:

Genesis 34:1-31—*Instead of waiting for his sons to come home (34:5), Jacob could have taken the initiative to seek justice from Hamor and Shechem or the people of their city. Moreover, instead of passively allowing his sons to address the marriage proposal (34:13-17), Jacob, as Dinah's father, could have made the arrangements with Hamor and Shechem himself and thus avoided his sons' deceitful plan.*

Genesis 37:2-36—*Instead of giving only his beloved Joseph the special robe (37:3), Jacob could have given all his sons special tokens of his love for them. In addition, Jacob could have taken Joseph's dreams seriously (37:10) but cautioned him against repeating them and, in so doing, creating problems with his brothers. Finally, since Joseph had already conveyed unfavorable reports on his brothers (37:2), Jacob might have had Joseph help tend the flocks instead of sending him to check on and report about his brothers (37:12-14).*

After eight minutes, ask one Genesis 34 group to read its Scripture up to the first turning point and then summarize what Jacob did and what happened as a result of his actions. Then have all the Genesis 34 groups read their new endings. Repeat the process with any other Genesis 34 turning points, then have the Genesis 37 groups present their findings in a similar way.

When both passages have been presented, explain that Genesis 49 records Jacob's deathbed blessing on and predictions about his sons. Read Genesis 49:5-7, 22-26. Then lead into the next section of the lesson by reading or restating the following in your own words: **"Because Jacob did not actively guide his children to do what was right, he struggled with their behavior. Because Jacob showed favoritism to one of his children, he struggled to keep sibling rivalry from tearing his family apart. But these were not Jacob's only struggles as a parent. Because Jacob did not handle these behavioral and relational problems when and as he should have, he also struggled with his children's future. By that time it was too late for Jacob, but it's not too late for us. We can learn from Jacob's struggles to prepare our children for the future by firmly and lovingly guiding each one in the present. So let's close today's lesson by discussing how to do that in the weeks and months to come."**

The Root of the Problem

Time: 15-18 minutes

Give each person a copy of the "Parenting Problems" handout and a pencil. Have people form groups of four or five, making sure to include both parents and

Materials Needed

☙ Bibles, photocopies of the "Parenting Problems" handout from page 42, photocopies of the **Scripture Commentary,** pencils

people without children in each group. Assign half the groups Genesis 34:1-31 and the other half Genesis 37:2-36. (If you prefer, work through the handout as a large group or have people complete it individually.) Make copies of the **Scripture Commentary** available for people to use.

Remind learners that they can learn even from the Bible's portrayal of negative examples, so they are to follow the instructions on the handout to learn the causes of misbehavior by and sibling rivalry among Jacob's children. After eight minutes, they will report what they learn to the entire class.

Circulate from group to group as people work, answering questions and guiding the discussion to ensure that people discover the following points.

Genesis 34:1-31—*Jacob's example shows that one cause of misconduct is parental inactivity and silence (not guiding children to proper behavior and not confronting them with sin as an offense against God).*

Genesis 37:2-36—*Jacob's struggles demonstrate that sibling rivalry can be caused by parental favoritism (visibly showing one's preference for one child) and parental inactivity (allowing one child to plant seeds of jealousy).*

After eight minutes, ask one Genesis 34 group to briefly summarize the story for the rest of the class. Then have all the Genesis 34 groups take turns reporting their answers to the questions. Repeat the process with the Genesis 37 groups.

When both passages have been presented, explain that Genesis 49 records Jacob's deathbed blessing on and predictions about his sons. Read Genesis 49:5-7, 22-26. Then lead into the next section of the lesson by reading or restating the following in your own words: **"Because Jacob did not actively guide his children to do what was right, he struggled with their behavior. Because Jacob showed favoritism to one of his children, he struggled to keep sibling rivalry from tearing his family apart. But these were not Jacob's only struggles as a parent. Because Jacob did not handle these behavioral and relational problems when and as he should have, he also struggled with his children's future. By that time it was too late for Jacob, but it's not too late for us. We can learn from Jacob's struggles to prepare our children for the future by firmly and lovingly guiding them in the present. So let's close our lesson by talking about how we can do just that in the weeks and months to come."**

PINNING IT DOWN . . .

Use one or both of the following activities to encourage class members to apply the truths of this lesson to modern struggles similar to Jacob's.

Modern Stories

Time: 12-15 minutes

Before class, cut out four to six newspaper articles that describe behavioral and relational struggles that parents have with their children today. (If you prefer, cut out

Materials Needed

↦ *articles from a current newspaper or magazine*

one article for every four or five class members and have students discuss the articles in small groups.)

Explain that Jacob's struggles with his children reveal, albeit in a negative way, that parents can best prepare their children for the future by practicing tough love with them. Parents need to offer their children strong guidance to do what is right and total affection for each and every child.

Then read the first newspaper article and ask learners to answer the following questions:

- **In what ways is this story similar to Jacob's struggles? How is it different?**
- **How do parents today follow Jacob's negative example in this situation?**
- **How could parents practice tough love with their kids in this situation?**

Allow several minutes for discussion, then repeat the process with the other stories.

Then ask each person to silently think of a child, whether their own or a child they care about, who struggles with behavioral or relational problems. After thirty seconds, challenge learners to think of how they could use the truths of this lesson to prepare that child for the future. For example, a father might decide to confront his children's misconduct instead of passively letting someone else deal with it. A mother might commit to praising each of her children equally. Someone without children might decide to share what he or she has learned with the parents of a special child.

Allow at least one minute for people to think, then read or restate the following prayer in your own words: **"Father, few things in life are so filled with promise and fraught with peril as raising children. But with your loving help and firm guidance, we can offer the same to the children we love. I ask that you help everyone here to keep the commitment to offer strong guidance and total affection to each and every child with whom he or she comes into contact. In Jesus' name, amen."**

Then move on to the next section or close the lesson by reminding students that the best way to prepare children for the future is by giving them the firm and loving guidance that they need in the present.

The Follow-Through Factor

Time: 5 minutes

This section appears in every lesson in this series. This weekly devotion plan helps class members apply the Bible study throughout the coming week. You may use it immediately after the Bible study or in conjunction with the preceding activity.

Give each person a copy of the handout. Take time to briefly read through it, but do not discuss any of the questions at this time.

Close the session in prayer.

Materials Needed

↪ *one copy of "The Follow-Through Factor" handout from page 43 for each person*

ACROSTIC ASPIRATIONS

The following clues describe hopes and dreams that people have for one particular category of loved ones. Solve the crossword-type clues below, then transfer the first letter from each answer into its corresponding blank below to reveal the loved ones to whom these aspirations apply.

1. Ability to stand on one's own feet __ __ __ __ __ __ __ __ __ __ __ __ __

2. Income tax term for children __ __ __ __ __ __ __ __ __ __ __

3. Ability to feel another's emotions __ __ __ __ __ __ __

4. Ready money __ __ __ __

5. Absence of abnormality __ __ __ __ __ __ __ __

6. Dependability __ __ __ __ __ __ __ __ __ __ __ __ __ __

7. Absence of sickness __ __ __ __ __ __

8. One of the three virtues (1 Corinthians 13:13) __ __ __ __

$$\overline{}\ \overline{}\ \overline{}\ \overline{}\ \overline{}\ \overline{}\ \overline{}\ \overline{}$$
  4   7   1   8   2   6   3   5

PARENTING PROBLEMS

Read your assigned passage and answer the corresponding questions below. Use the insights from the **Scripture Commentary** as needed. Also, jot down any questions or insights you have concerning your passage.

Genesis 34:1-31

- How did Jacob's silence (v. 5) and inactivity (vv. 6-17) contribute to his sons' evil deeds?

- How do you think Jacob should have responded to the rape of Dinah? to his sons' deeds?

- What does Jacob's rebuke of Simeon and Levi (v. 30) reveal about his main concerns?

- In one sentence, what does this passage teach about a cause of misconduct by children?

Genesis 37:2-36

- What were the different causes of the sibling rivalry between Joseph and his brothers?

- If God gave Joseph these dreams (vv. 5-10), how should Jacob have dealt with them?

- What do you think Jacob could have done to prevent this sibling rivalry? to minimize it?

- In one sentence, what does this passage teach about a cause of sibling rivalry among children?

THE FOLLOW-THROUGH FACTOR

Jacob struggled in his relationships with his children.

Consider the implications of your last Bible study throughout the next week.

Monday
Read Genesis 34:1-7 and John 2:13-16.
What does Jacob's reaction (or lack thereof) imply about his relationship with his daughter? his toleration of sin? What children-damaging sins does today's society tolerate? today's church tolerate?

Tuesday
Read Genesis 34:8-31 and Matthew 26:47-54.
How do you think Simeon and Levi should have responded to Shechem's rape of their sister? Why do you think Jesus rejects violence as a means of advancing God's plan? How can you overcome the influence of violence in your life? in the lives of children?

Wednesday
Read Genesis 37:2-11 and James 2:1-9.
Did God's decision to elevate Joseph justify Jacob's tendency to do the same? Why or why not? Think of one person (or child) you like one and you don't like as well. What steps can you take to make sure that you treat everyone equally well?

Thursday
Read Genesis 37:12-36 and Ephesians 5:8-11.
How would you evaluate Reuben's and Judah's attempts to save Joseph's life? What else could they have done to protect Joseph? to save their father grief? How can the church today protect children? strengthen parents?

Friday
Read Genesis 49:1-7, 14-17, 27 and Exodus 34:6, 7.
How did these sons' past sins shape their own futures? those of their children? How have you been affected by your parents' sins? What can you keep from perpetuating this cycle of sin?

Saturday
Read Genesis 49:8-13, 18-26, 28 and Deuteronomy 28:1-14.
How has God blessed you through your parents? other family members? How might you act as a source of blessing for your children or other family members?

LESSON 5
Jacob struggled with tragedy and death.

LESSON SCRIPTURE

Genesis 35:16-29; 37:12-35; 47:1-12; 48:1-9

SCRIPTURE COMMENTARY

We may face many difficulties and losses: broken relationships, financial setbacks, pain, sickness, even death. Yet, because we have God's resurrection power working within us, we have the ability to triumph through every one of them. Three incidents from the life of Jacob can show us how.

Jacob struggled with the deaths of his wife and of his father— Within the space of fourteen short verses (Genesis 35:16-29), Jacob lost two of the most important people in his life: his beloved wife Rachel (cf. Genesis 29:30) and his father, Isaac. The death of Isaac probably was no great shock. He was, after all, "old and full of years" (35:29). But Rachel died during the prime of life, during the act of giving life to a son. Jacob, the object of God's love and the bearer of his promise, had to face the reality of death and loss.

Still, Jacob could cope with his losses by focusing his attention on all that he had gained. For example, Jacob renamed the son whose birth had caused the death of his wife. Rachel, with good reason, had named the boy Ben-Oni, "son of my trouble" in Hebrew. Jacob, however, chose to look beyond the trouble the child had caused and gave him a new name: Benjamin, "son of my right hand." Jacob grieved the loss of Rachel, to be sure, and kept her memory alive with a suitable memorial (35:20), but he also drew strength and solace from the life God had created with the death of his wife.

Other evidence supports the idea that Jacob dealt with his losses by recalling all that God had given him. At first glance, a reader might think that the placement of Genesis 35:23-26 is strange, a record of sons born sandwiched between the report of two deaths. However, it may be that the biblical author is reminding us (as God had earlier reminded Jacob, cf. Genesis 33:4, 5) that God had been generous to Jacob, that his long-term gains (twelve sons) far outweighed his recent losses.

In sum, this biblical record of Jacob's struggles reveals an important principle for dealing with loss. One way we can overcome the tragic losses we face is by recalling all the good things God has graciously brought our way. Those who can maintain a balanced perspective in the midst of great loss will eventually rise above their losses to celebrate God's life even in the presence of death.

Lesson Objectives

In the course of this lesson, students will
- *recognize that they will inevitably lose someone or something important to them.*
- *describe how Jacob encountered and handled the realities of death.*
- *deal with or prepare for their own losses.*

Jacob struggled with the loss of a son—Genesis 37:12-35 reveals another piece of the puzzle for dealing with loss. Important as it is to keep one's perspective during the pain of great loss, it is not enough. Like Jacob in this passage, we must also take time to mourn the one we lost.

It is interesting to note here, however, that the loss Jacob experienced was not as real or as final as he presumed. Granted, Jacob had, for all practical purposes, lost Joseph, his most-loved son (Genesis 37:3). But Jacob's loss was more apparent than real, and he would again see this treasured son (cf. 46:28-30). As those who live with the hope of resurrection, we would do well to remember this when we lose those we love.

Still, Jacob's *experience* of loss was real, and he reacted in an entirely appropriate way: he wept (37:35). In keeping with the custom of his day, Jacob ripped the hem of his robe, possibly to signify that his life had been "torn" in two. Jacob also put on the traditional sackcloth, a coarse, often black, material made of goat or camel hair that symbolized discomfort after the death of a loved one.

Finally, Jacob refused to be comforted during his time of mourning (35:35). Jacob knew that this was a time to weep. In the face of such tragedy and loss, anything less would be an insult to his lost son. From Jacob's actions we learn that it is acceptable, even necessary, to honestly mourn our losses. Perspective is important, in time, but first we must grieve that which we have lost.

Jacob struggled with coming to the end of his own life—Because Jacob had dealt with his losses in a healthy way, mourning them as was fitting and then regaining his perspective about God's goodness, he was able to rise above the fear of his own death and actually use it as an occasion to bless others.

Jacob was an old man by the time he finally arrived in Egypt to be reunited with his long-lost son, Joseph (cf. Genesis 46:28-30). He knew that he too, like those who had gone before him, soon would die. Jacob could have raged "against the dying of the light," but he chose rather to go gently and graciously into the night.

Two incidents especially highlight Jacob's grace in the face of death. Genesis 47:1-10, for example, describes how Jacob blessed Pharaoh, a foreign king he barely knew. Jacob held no illusions about the course of his life. It had been a struggle throughout and was now rapidly (and all too soon, cf. 47:9) drawing to an end. Yet Jacob refused to wallow in bitterness. Instead, he blessed Pharaoh twice and then went his way.

In a similar way, Jacob also took time to bless Joseph's two sons even as he lay on his deathbed (48:1-9; see also 48:21, 22; 49:1-28). Instead of demanding that others care for his crushing needs, Jacob graciously transformed his imminent loss into gain for others. Thus one can learn from Jacob's example one final principle for overcoming death and loss: After we genuinely mourn and then regain perspective concerning our losses, we should use those losses as a channel of God's blessing to others.

As long as Christians are in this world, they will have to experience and endure tragic losses. But as those who have the truth of God's Word and the power of God's resurrection life within them, they can overcome any loss and actually turn it into something good. ✤

Hebrew Helps

Jacob set up a "matstsebah" over Rachel's tomb (35:20). This word simply means "a thing set up" and can refer to anything from a simple memorial (as in this case) to a pagan image (Deuteronomy 7:5; 1 Kings 14:23).

This is the last of three "matstsebah" set up by Jacob during his life. The first was the stone on which he slept at Bethel when he was fleeing the wrath of Esau. At that place Jehovah demonstrated his presence in the vision of a stairway reaching to Heaven (28:18, 22). The second was set up at Mizpah, signifying the stressful dissolution of his working relationship with Laban. At that place Jacob trusted the Lord to continue to deliver him from the treachery of his father-in-law (31:45, 51, 52). Now he recalls the blessings of his marriage to his true love.

While we may not choose to set up physical pillars, Jacob's example provides us a model for dealing with life's transitions. We should recognize the grace God has provided before a time of great stress and ask for his continued presence.

GETTING A HOLD . . .

Use one of the following activities to help class members recognize that they will inevitably lose someone or something important to them.

Sudden Losses

Time: 10-12 minutes

When everyone has arrived, give each person three index cards and a pencil or pen. Invite people to write on their cards the three most important people in their lives, one person per card.

Allow a minute or so for people to write, then ask people to form groups of four or five. Then have group members each take a minute to tell each other why these three people are so important to them.

When everyone has had a chance to talk, direct people to hold their three cards out in front of them. Then instruct group members to each take one card from the person on his or her left.

After the cards have been taken away, explain to class members that the people we treasure most in our lives can be taken away just as quickly (and randomly) as the cards they just lost. In fact, one of life's few certainties is that eventually every person present will experience some sort of loss.

Then ask group members to discuss the following questions:

- **What is the most painful loss you have experienced in your life?**
- **What did you do or could you have done to overcome that loss?**
- **What important person or thing in life do you most fear losing?**
- **How do you think you would react if you lost that person or thing?**

Then read or summarize in your own words the following transition into the Bible study: **"Much as we might want to ignore it, the hard truth is that life is filled with losses. People lose money, houses, jobs, friendships— even opportunities that they will never have again. Hardest of all, sooner or later we will all lose someone we dearly love. Eventually we will all have to face the death of a parent, a friend, a spouse, maybe even a child. And even though we all recognize that these losses are inevitable, we are never fully prepared for them when they happen to us. We can, however, learn from the biblical example of Jacob how we might cope better when we are faced with the losses that will undoubtedly come our way."**

The Awful Truth

Time: 7-10 minutes

When everyone has arrived, remind students of all the difficulties that Jacob struggled to overcome in his life: poor relationships with his parents and brother, marital disappointments and difficulties, business troubles, and strained relations with his children. Then explain that, as difficult as these problems were, there was one struggle Jacob had to face that was far worse than all of these. That difficulty is the subject of today's lesson.

Give each person a copy of the "The Awful Truth" handout and a pen or pencil. Explain that the difficulty Jacob faced will become apparent as students unscramble the sentences on the handout. (If you prefer, have learners work together in small groups to unscramble the sentences.)

Allow several minutes for people to unscramble the sentences, then ask them to read the quotes they discovered. The sentences should read as follows:

- *In this world nothing can be said to be certain except death and taxes.*
- *To every man upon this earth death cometh soon or late.*
- *Because I could not stop for Death he kindly stopped for me.*
- *He who's not busy being born is busy dying.*
- *For all can see that wise men die; the foolish and the senseless alike perish.*

Then ask the entire class: **"What truth do all these quotes have in common?"** (They all claim that death is inevitable. Sooner or later, everyone dies.) **"To what extent do you agree with these quotes? disagree with them?"**

Then invite everyone to write at the bottom of the handout the name of one person whose death he or she had to face. Allow thirty seconds for people to write, then ask them each to write the name of a living loved one whose death would be difficult to cope with.

After a minute, lead into the Bible study by reading or restating the following in your own words: **"God's Word says that, unless Jesus returns beforehand, everyone is destined to die. It happened to the person you've already lost; it will happen to the loved one whose name you just wrote down. It will even happen to you. And even though we all know this awful truth, we are never completely prepared for it when it happens to us. We can, however, learn from the biblical example of Jacob how we might cope better when we are faced with the loss that death will undoubtedly bring our way."**

TAKING IT TO THE MAT . . .

Use one of the following activities to help people describe how Jacob encountered and handled the realities of death.

Dear Diary

Time: 15-18 minutes

Ask people to form groups of four or five (or keep people in their groups from the opening activity). Give each group a copy of the **Scripture Commentary**, paper, and a pencil.

Assign each group one of the following passages: Genesis 35:16-29; Genesis 37:12-35; and Genesis 47:1-12; 48:1-9, 21, 22. Explain that group members are to read the assigned passage together to discover:

Materials Needed

↦ *Bibles, photocopies of the **Scripture Commentary**, paper, and pencils*

- *the specific loss or losses that Jacob faced.*
- *how he felt about that loss.*
- *how he coped with or overcame that loss.*

Then students are to put themselves in Jacob's place and write a diary entry that Jacob might have written sometime after his loss. The diary entry should record what had happened, Jacob's emotional state after his loss, and how Jacob coped with or overcame the loss he experienced.

Allow groups ten minutes to study the Scripture and write their entries. While people work, move from group to group to answer any questions and offer needed guidance. Offer suggestions to ensure that learners discover the following points:

Genesis 35:16-29—*Sandwiched between the deaths of his beloved Rachel and his father Isaac, Jacob was reminded of all the good things God had given him, namely, his children.*

Genesis 37:12-35—*When Jacob came to think that Joseph was dead, he gave full and honest expression to his grief. He did not deny or hide his anguish even when others tried to comfort him.*

Genesis 47:1-10; 48:1-9, 21, 22—*As Jacob approached the inevitable end of his hard life, he used it as an opportunity to bless others, including a pharaoh he barely knew as well as the members of his own family.*

After ten minutes, ask for volunteers to read their groups' entries to the entire class. When all the diary entries have been read, ask the entire class the following questions:

- **What might have happened if Jacob had never grieved his losses? if he had only grieved them?**
- **What does this teach us about the best way to deal with *and* to overcome our losses?**
- **How did Jacob's honest grief and his recognition of God's blessings help him bless others?**

Then lead into the next part of the lesson by reading or restating the following in your own words: **"The life of Jacob offers us several examples of how God's people can cope with and overcome the loss of loved ones. Like all people, we mourn the passing of friends and family. But we can also see the hand of God's blessing in our lives—even in the face of death. Finally, like Jacob, we can grow through the losses we face and turn the experience of loss into an expression of blessing to others. Let's conclude our lesson by seeing how we can put that into practice in our daily lives."**

Stages of Growth

Time: 18-20 minutes

Explain to class members that psychologists have identified five stages that most people facing a terminal illness go through: denial, anger, bargaining, grieving, and acceptance. Invite students to define or give an illustration of each stage. Then ask: **"Why do you think people often go through four stages before they**

Materials Needed

↝ *Bibles, one copy of the "Stages of Growth" handout from page 52 for each person, copies of the **Scripture Commentary**, pencils or pens*

reach the final stage, acceptance? Do you think Christians generally go through these stages? Why or why not?"

Then explain to people that, because Christians have the power of God working in them, they can do more than come to grips with their losses—they can actually *grow* through them. Three incidents from the life of Jacob offer a good example of how we can not only deal with our losses but also grow through them.

Give each person a copy of the "Stages of Growth" handout and a pencil. Set out copies of the **Scripture Commentary.** Inform people that they have twelve minutes to finish the handout (using their Bibles and the **Scripture Commentary** as needed), after which they will share their results with the entire class. (If you prefer, people can work together in small groups and you can assign each part of the handout to a different group.)

While people work, make yourself available to answer questions and offer help. Be sure to periodically remind people of the time remaining.

After ten minutes, ask for volunteers to report what they discovered. Guide the discussion as necessary to ensure that the following ideas are brought out—Stage 1: mourn our losses; Stage 2: regain our perspective; Stage 3: use our losses for others' gain. Then ask the entire class the following questions:

- **What might have happened if Jacob had never mourned? if he had not seen God's blessings?**
- **What does this teach us about the best way to deal with *and* to grow through our losses?**
- **How did Jacob's honest grief and the recognition of God's blessings help him bless others?**

Then lead into the next part of the lesson by reading or restating the following in your own words: **"The life of Jacob offers us several examples of how God's people can cope with and overcome the loss of loved ones. Like all people, we mourn the passing of friends and family. But we can also see the hand of God's blessing in our lives—even in the face of death. Finally, like Jacob, we can grow through the losses we face and turn the experience of loss into an expression of blessing to others. Let's conclude our lesson by seeing how we can put that into practice in our daily lives."**

PINNING IT DOWN . . .

Use one or both of the following activities to encourage learners to deal with or to prepare for their own losses.

Now You See It

Time: 12-15 minutes

Before class, blow up and tie off all but two of the balloons. Then place one of the remaining balloons inside the other and inflate both at the same time, making

Materials Needed

↦ *one balloon for each class member plus five extras, a straight pin, markers* sure to inflate the outside balloon slightly larger than the inside one. During class, you will use the straight pin to prick the top of the outside balloon without popping the balloon inside. (You may want to practice this trick several times before class so you can perform it easily later on.)

Set out the balloons, making sure to remember which one is the double balloon. Then read the following, popping a balloon with the straight pin as indicated: **"Life is much like a balloon—fragile and extremely frail** (pop a balloon). **We may banish thoughts of death from our minds, but sooner or later our bubble will burst** (pop a balloon) **and death will intrude on our lives. No matter what we do, we and those we love will all eventually and inevitably die** (pop a balloon). **But as Christians we need not fear death, for we have God's resurrection power living in us. In fact, we can confidently celebrate life even in the face of death** (pop the outside balloon of the double balloon), **for we know that the living God will give us the ability to overcome death, both now and in the resurrection life to come."**

Toss out the balloons and pass out the markers until everyone has one. Instruct class members to each draw on the balloon the face of someone whose death they are still dealing with or a loved one whose death would be difficult to cope with.

Allow several minutes for people to draw, then ask students to form groups of four or five. Ask each group member to identify who the balloon represents and to explain why he or she drew that person's face.

When everyone has shared, invite group members to help each other think of one thing they can do to apply the lesson to their situations, whether by mourning or regaining perspective about the loss of a loved one or by being a blessing to a loved one who is still alive.

After five minutes of discussion, have group members close by praying for each other's commitments. Then move on to the next section or conclude the lesson by encouraging students to take their balloons home as a reminder to celebrate God's resurrection life by following the example of Jacob even in the face of death.

The Follow-Through Factor

Time: 5 minutes

This section appears in every lesson in this series. This weekly devotion plan helps class members apply the Bible study throughout the coming week. You may use it immediately after the Bible study or in conjunction with the preceding activity.

Give each person a copy of the handout. Take time to briefly read through it, but do not discuss any of the questions at this time.

Close the session in prayer.

Materials Needed

⟿ one copy of "The Follow-Through Factor" handout from page 53 for each person

THE AWFUL TRUTH

Unscramble the following quotes and then write them in their proper order. See how many you can finish in three minutes.

1. and be be can certain death except in nothing said taxes this to world. (Benjamin Franklin)

_____

2. cometh death earth every late man or soon this to upon. (Lord Macaulay)

_____

3. because could death for for he I kindly me not stop stopped. (Emily Dickinson)

_____

4. being born busy busy dying he is not who's. (Bob Dylan)

_____

5. alike all and can die; foolish for men perish see senseless that the the wise. (Psalm 49:10)

_____

STAGES OF GROWTH

Read each Scripture passage below and, using the **Scripture Commentary** as needed, briefly answer the questions below each passage.

STAGE 1: *GENESIS 37:12-35*

- According to verses 34 and 35, how did Jacob react to the loss of his son?

- Why do you think Jacob refused to be comforted by his other children?

- What does this teach us about the first step in growing through our losses?

STAGE 2: *GENESIS 35:16-29*

- What is the significance of Jacob renaming the son Rachel had already named?

- Why do you think the list of Jacob's sons appears between the two death reports?

- What does this teach us about how we can move past the stage of mourning?

STAGE 3: *GENESIS 47:1-10; 48:1-9, 21, 22*

- How do you think Jacob viewed his life thus far? his approaching death?

- Why do you think Jacob wanted to bless Pharaoh and his family at this time?

- What does Jacob's example teach us about how we should react to our losses?

THE FOLLOW-THROUGH FACTOR

Jacob struggled with tragedy and death.

Consider the implications of your last Bible study throughout the next week.

Monday ***Read Genesis 35:16-20, 27-29 and Romans 8:28-39.*** Why is the death of a loved one so difficult to accept? How have you struggled with the death of someone you love? How can the assurance of God's love help you face the inevitable deaths of those you love?	
Tuesday ***Read Genesis 35:23-26 and Psalm 127:1-5.*** How might the blessing of children have helped Jacob to cope with his losses? What losses have you endured in your life? Who are two "blessings" God has given you?	
Wednesday ***Read Genesis 37:12-28 and 50:15-21. (If you have time, also scan Genesis 38–41.)*** What losses did Joseph face in his life? How did these losses affect his relationship with God? with his brothers? How might you imitate Joseph's example with a loss you have recently faced or are currently facing?	
Thursday ***Read Genesis 37:29-35 and Ecclesiastes 3:1-4.*** Why do you think Jacob refused to be comforted? When do you think it is proper to mourn? When might it be inappropriate or unhealthy to mourn?	
Friday ***Read Genesis 47:1-10 and John 16:33.*** Based on what you know about Jacob, what kind of difficulties do you think he had in mind in verse 9? What are the two most pressing difficulties you face right now? How might Jacob's experiences or Jesus' promise help you face and overcome those difficulties?	
Saturday ***Read Genesis 48:1-9 and John 17.*** Why do you think Jacob wanted to bless others as he drew nearer to his own death? If you knew you were going to die in one month, what would you want to do before you died?	

LESSON 6

Jacob struggled in his relationship with God.

LESSON SCRIPTURE

Genesis 28:10-22; 32:1-32; 35:1-15

SCRIPTURE COMMENTARY

All of Jacob's struggles in life stemmed, in one way or another, from his life-long struggle with God. In the end, he learned how to increase his trust in God and, in so doing, improved his relationships with others. His experiences can teach us how to do the same.

Jacob struggled with allowing God to direct his life—Jacob had been born under a promise of God (see Genesis 25:23-26), but because he did not trust God to make good on that promise, he spent the first years of his life striving to gain it on his own. He took advantage of Esau's weakness to seize his brother's first right of inheritance and even deceived and lied to his father to grasp the blessing intended for Esau (25:27-34; 27:1-29). As a result of Jacob's strivings, he was eventually forced to leave his family and flee for his life (27:41–28:5). It was as Jacob was running that he first encountered God and began, ever so slightly, to trust him to direct his life.

Genesis 28:10-22 records that encounter, and it reveals several important lessons on increasing one's trust in God. We should first note that Jacob's trust in God began to grow when he encountered God's word for himself. Jacob's dream-vision of God was undoubtedly important and impressive, but his direct contact with God's word stands at the center of this narrative and of Jacob's change in heart. One might even suggest that Jacob's previous lack of faith stemmed from his secondhand knowledge of God's promise. When Jacob heard God's word for himself, however, he began to trust God to direct his life.

Of course, Jacob's faith in the God of Abraham and Isaac (28:13) was small at the beginning. God would be his God *only* if he met certain conditions (25:20, 21). Still, Jacob had heard from God's own mouth that he (and not Jacob) would be the one to fulfill the promise (observe how often God repeats "I will" in verses 13-15), and that seemed to plant the seed of faith in his heart and to convince him to stop trying to usurp the place of God in fulfilling the promise. Thus we learn from this narrative that faith begins with an encounter with God's Word, an encounter that leads one to trust God to direct the course of his or her life.

Lesson Objectives

In the course of this lesson, students will
- ✧ discover what makes it difficult for people to trust God.
- ✧ describe how Jacob grew in his ability to trust God.
- ✧ commit to increasing their trust in God in one of three ways.

Jacob struggled with trusting that God would keep his word—Jacob continued to struggle in the years following his first encounter with God, but one can see growth in his faith. In Genesis 32:1-32, Jacob appears to have progressed from a conditional faith to a fearful but persevering faith.

As Jacob journeyed back to meet his fate, to meet his previously furious brother Esau, he knew that God was journeying with him (32:1). Still, Jacob feared that God might not keep his earlier word, the promise to protect him from harm (28:15). It is even plausible that Jacob's careful preparations for the meeting (32:13-21) betray the weakness of his faith.

Still, Jacob eventually overcame his fears (and thus increased his faith) in three specific ways. First, he addressed his concerns directly to God in prayer (32:9-12). In his prayer he admitted his fears and asked for God's protection. Second, within his prayer Jacob reminded God (and himself) of the promise that he had made. When Jacob's faith started to waver, he recalled God's promise and petitioned God to keep his word.

Finally, Jacob also deepened his faith by persevering through his struggles. The details of Jacob's nighttime wrestling match are somewhat vague (see sidebar), but its meaning is crystal clear. Jacob had "struggled with God and with men and [had] overcome" (32:28). Jacob's faith grew stronger through a direct and persevering encounter with God himself. In the same way, we can also deepen our faith by persevering in our direct interaction with God through prayer.

Jacob struggled with committing himself completely to God—Jacob's faith had grown tremendously since his first encounter with God, but he still had room for growth (as do all people). Thus, it is not surprising to note that his third meeting with God (Genesis 35:1-15) deepened Jacob's faith in two specific ways.

Jacob was by no means perfect, as the presence of idols within his family clearly shows (35:2-4). But when God ordered Jacob to go to Bethel, he immediately obeyed (35:1, 6). In contrast to his earlier self-willed behavior, Jacob now submitted himself to God's will without argument and without delay.

In addition, Jacob also removed everything (the foreign gods) that stood in the way of wholehearted commitment to God (35:2-4). As a result, Jacob was prepared not only to meet God (35:9-13) but also to worship God as *his* God (35:14, 15). Jacob had learned, through the experiences and struggles of his life, to trust God fully as his only Lord. Thus we learn from Jacob that we can develop and deepen our faith by committing ourselves completely to him in worship and obedience.

Throughout his life Jacob struggled to trust God not only for his future but also during the course of his day-to-day existence. His struggles teach us that we too can increase our trust in God through our direct contact with God's Word, our personal encounter with God in persevering prayer, and our wholehearted commitment to obey and worship God as our only true and trustworthy God. ✤

Further Insight

Jacob's combatant seemed to be just a man, but his dislocation of Jacob's hip (32:25) reveals supernatural or divine power. Also, this "man's" comment that Jacob had struggled with God (32:28) and Jacob's assertion that he had seen God "face to face" would seem to indicate that Jacob had actually wrestled with God. It appears that this conflict was designed by God as a powerful illustration to Jacob. The fearful Jacob's confidence would grow when realizing that while he may emerge scarred, he could prevail in the most difficult of conflicts.

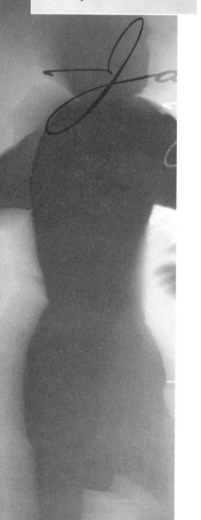

GETTING A HOLD . . .

Use one of the following activities to help students discover what makes it difficult to trust God.

Materials Needed

↦ cardboard box, four or five blindfolds, four or five "living" items such as plants or Bibles

Trust Me

Time: 10-12 minutes

Before class, place your "living" items in the cardboard box and close it so no one can see inside. Set the box at the front of the room.

When everyone has arrived, ask for a volunteer to explain what a trust walk is. (It is a team-building activity in which a person leads a blindfolded partner around by the hand to increase the blindfolded person's ability to trust.) Ask class members who have participated in this exercise to briefly recount their experiences.

Then explain that you have a different sort of trust test that you would like four or five volunteers to help you with. As in the trust walk, the volunteers will wear blindfolds, but in this activity they will need to trust you to place something in their outstretched hands. All that you can say about the item is that it is alive but will not physically harm them.

If people are hesitant to volunteer, keep asking them, **"What's the matter? Don't you trust me?"** Keep prodding people in a good-natured manner until you have the volunteers. Ask others to help blindfold the volunteers, then have the volunteers stand at the front of the room, with arms outstretched, as you set the items in their hands. (For added fun, heighten the drama with comments such as, **"Can someone keep the others in the box while I take care of this one?"** or **"Don't let him get away."**)

After you have placed the items in the volunteers' hands, remove the blindfolds, thank them for their help, and announce that they can keep their items.

Then ask the entire group: **"Why were some of you hesitant to volunteer for this activity?"** *I didn't know what you might put in my hands. I don't like not being able to see what's going on.* **"How is this trust exercise like trusting God every day of our lives?"** *We often don't know what God is going to do. We can't see God or what he is doing.*

Then read or summarize in your own words the following transition into the Bible study: **"Odds are, we have all been disappointed by someone whom we placed our trust in, perhaps by a friend who took advantage of us or a family member who didn't do what he or she promised to do. And that makes it difficult to trust others, even God. But like one of these plants, trust can grow and blossom. We simply need to make sure that we follow the right 'care instructions,' which are found in God's Word."**

Materials Needed

↦ one photocopy of the "Measure of Trust" handout from page 61 for each person, pens or pencils

A Measure of Trust

Time: 7-10 minutes

As people arrive, give them a copy of the "Measure of Trust" handout and a pen or pencil. Instruct class members to read the directions at the top of the handout and then complete the "trust" evaluation that follows.

When everyone has arrived and most have finished the handout, invite people to report their scores. (If you would like, record the scores on a chalkboard or a sheet of newsprint so everyone can see the range of scores.) Then ask the entire class the following questions:

- **Which of the situations received high scores on your evaluation? low scores?**
- **Why would you have difficulty trusting the people who received low scores?**
- **What do our overall scores reveal about our willingness to trust other people?**
- **How do you think a lack of trust in others affects our willingness to trust God?**
- **Why do you think it is difficult for people to trust God every day of their lives?**

Then read or summarize in your own words the following transition into the Bible study: **"In all likelihood, we've all been disappointed by untrustworthy people, and not just politicians, advertising agents, or employers. At some time or another, we all have experienced a betrayal of trust from a family member, a friend, or even a Christian leader. Unfortunately, that makes it even harder for us to trust God. Still, we can learn how to trust God more. Jacob did, and as we apply the insights we learn from his life, we can too."**

TAKING IT TO THE MAT . . .

Use one of the following activities to help people describe how Jacob grew in his ability to trust God.

Jacob's Progress

Time: 18-20 minutes

Before class, write the following questions on newsprint:
- **How did God communicate with Jacob?**
- **What exactly did God say or do to Jacob?**
- **How did Jacob respond to this encounter?**
- **What does this reveal about Jacob's faith?**

To begin, spend a few minutes reminding students how Jacob ("the grasper") had earlier taken advantage of Esau's weakness to gain the first right of inheritance and then lied to his father to steal the blessing intended for Esau. Ask class members to discuss what those two incidents reveal about Jacob's level of trust in God to fulfill his word (see also Genesis 25:21-23).

Materials Needed

↦ *Bibles, photocopies of the **Scripture Commentary**, paper, pen or pencils, newsprint, a marker, tape*

Then explain to class members that, although Jacob began with little or no trust in God at the beginning of his life, he developed a strong confidence in God through three separate incidents in which he encountered God.

Divide the class into three groups. Give each group paper, a pen or pencil, and a photocopy of the **Scripture Commentary.** Hang the newsprint with questions where everyone can see it. Assign each group one of these passages: Genesis 28:10-22; 32:1-32; 35:1-15. Explain that each group will evaluate its passage to answer the questions listed on the newsprint. After eight minutes, groups will compare their answers to discover how Jacob's trust in God increased.

While people work, circulate among the groups to answer any questions and to make sure that the insights discussed in the **Scripture Commentary** come through.

After eight minutes, have groups present their discoveries in the order of their passages. Then ask the entire class the following questions, using the suggested responses to guide the discussion:

- **How did Jacob's trust in God increase after each encounter with God?** *First he made a conditional commitment to God, then he prayed to and struggled with God, and finally he obeyed and worshiped God as his only God.*
- **Why do you think God's contact with Jacob became less "spectacular" with each encounter?** *As Jacob's trust in God increased, his need for "spectacular" experiences decreased. God encountered him more naturally, in the course of his daily life.*
- **How would you describe the stages of Jacob's progress in faith?** *Jacob first began to trust God's promise, then he encountered God personally through prayer and his "struggle" with God's messenger, and finally he committed himself wholeheartedly to God.*

Then lead into the next part of the lesson by reading or restating the following in your own words: **"Jacob's trust in God slowly but steadily increased as he first heard God's promise, then encountered God personally in persevering prayer, and finally committed himself completely to obey and worship God. Our trust in God can also grow as we commit ourselves to learning God's Word, encountering God directly in prayer, and committing ourselves wholeheartedly to him."**

Faith on Trial

Time: 15-18 minutes

Before class, make one photocopy of the "Faith on Trial" handout for every four people.

Ask people to form groups of four or five. Explain that group members are to act as "grand jury members" given the task of determining whether or not Jacob trusted God. Give each group a copy of the "Faith on Trial" handout, a copy of the **Scripture Commentary,** and a pen or pencil. Direct groups to read and follow the directions at the top of the handout to fulfill their responsibility. Groups have twelve minutes to complete their task.

Move from group to group while students work, answering questions, offering suggestions, and reminding people of the time remaining.

After twelve minutes, invite groups to report their findings. Encourage a bit of friendly debate and discussion among class members. Comment as necessary to help students see that Jacob had faith in each case but that Jacob's trust in God grew from a conditional faith to a fearful but persevering faith and finally to a committed and obedient faith. Then ask the entire class the following questions:

- **What do Jacob's experiences imply about the nature of trusting God?** *Trust is something we need to develop over time.*

- **How would you describe the stages of Jacob's progress in faith?** *Jacob first began to trust God's promise, then he encountered God personally through prayer and his "struggle" with God's messenger, and finally he committed himself wholeheartedly to God.*

- **How can we apply Jacob's example to our own progress in faith?** *We begin by learning what God has said, grow through personal interaction with him, and then commit ourselves completely to obeying and worshiping him.*

Then lead into the next part of the lesson by reading or restating the following in your own words: **"Jacob's trust in God may have been weak at the beginning, but it grew stronger as he first heard God's promise, then encountered God personally in persevering prayer, and finally committed himself completely to obey and worship God. Our trust in God can also increase as we commit ourselves to learning God's Word, encountering God directly in prayer, and committing ourselves completely to him."**

PINNING IT DOWN . . .

Use one or both of the following activities to challenge learners to commit to increasing their trust in God in one of three ways.

O For Grace to Trust Him More

Time: 10-12 minutes

Ask students to listen carefully as you read aloud the words to the first verse and chorus of "'Tis So Sweet to Trust in Jesus." Then explain that the words of the hymn mirror Jacob's experience in several key ways. Read the first verse again, making the comments below as indicated:

> **'Tis so sweet to trust in Jesus,**
> **Just to take him at his word,** *Jacob's faith began when he first heard God's Word.*

Materials Needed

⤙ hymnals containing "'Tis So Sweet to Trust in Jesus," index cards, pens or pencils

Just to rest upon his promise, *Jacob's faith grew when he trusted God's promise to protect him from Esau.*

Just to know,
"Thus saith the Lord." *Jacob's faith finally blossomed when he committed himself to obeying what God had said*

Then distribute the hymnals and invite class members to sing the first verse and chorus with you as you all reflect about where you are on your faith journeys—just learning to trust, living with a mixture of faith and fear, or experiencing a life of full commitment and obedience to God.

After you sing through the song, remind people of its last words: "O for grace to trust him more." Remind learners that no matter how much they might trust God today, they still need to increase their trust in him.

Give each person an index card and a pen or pencil. Then challenge students to spend a few moments in quiet reflection, asking God to reveal where they actually are on their faith journeys (suggest that they relate them to the life of Jacob if need be) and what they can do to increase their trust in him, whether through learning his Word, spending time in intimate prayer with him, or obeying and worshiping him more fully. Challenge people to write out their commitments on the cards.

Allow students several minutes to reflect and record their commitments, then move on to the next section or close in prayer, asking God to give learners grace to increase their trust in him.

The Follow-Through Factor

Time: 5 minutes

This section appears in every lesson in this series. This weekly devotion plan helps class members apply the Bible study throughout the coming week. You may use it immediately after the Bible study or in conjunction with the preceding activity.

Give each person a copy of the handout. Take time to briefly read through it, but do not discuss any of the questions at this time.

Close the session in prayer.

Materials Needed

⤶ one copy of "The Follow-Through Factor" handout from page 63 for each person

A MEASURE OF TRUST

Read each statement below and rate how much you would trust the person making the claim. Circle 0 for "not on your life," 1 for "maybe, depending on how I felt that day," 2 for "sure, unless it was proven otherwise," and 3 for "I would bank my life on it." Then total your score at the bottom of the page.

1. A politician promises to trim taxes and reduce the national debt without cutting any essential services.
   0   1   2   3

2. A vitamin company claims that if you use its product, you will add five years to your life span.
   0   1   2   3

3. A televangelist vows that if you send him $20, you will experience God's blessing on your bank account.
   0   1   2   3

4. A teenage daughter promises to stop sneaking out at night to see a boyfriend you disapprove of.
   0   1   2   3

5. A newspaper claims that the police in your city shot an unarmed man because of his race.
   0   1   2   3

6. The police chief states that the shooting was fully justified because the man was endangering an officer.
   0   1   2   3

7. A neighbor promises to water your lawn and set out your garbage while you are on vacation.
   0   1   2   3

8. An employer promises to reward you at year's end if you will put in extra hours for three months.
   0   1   2   3

   Total score: ____

FAITH ON TRIAL

You are members of a grand jury investigating whether, in fact, Jacob trusted God. The only evidence you are to consider is that contained within the biblical passages listed below. Read each passage and answer the questions below it to help you form an opinion. You have twelve minutes to reach your verdict.

Genesis 28:10-22

- What evidence do you see that Jacob trusted God? that he didn't trust God?

- What did God do or say in this account that would warrant Jacob's trust?

- In your opinion, does the evidence support a claim that Jacob trusted God?

Genesis 32:1-32

- What evidence do you see that Jacob trusted God? that he didn't trust God?

- What did God do or say in this account that would warrant Jacob's trust?

- In your opinion, does the evidence support a claim that Jacob trusted God?

Genesis 35:1-15

- What evidence do you see that Jacob trusted God? that he didn't trust God?

- What did God do or say in this account that would warrant Jacob's trust?

- In your opinion, does the evidence support a claim that Jacob trusted God?